LEARNING DISABILITIES

FOUND IN ASSOCIATION WITH

FRENCH IMMERSION PROGRAMMING

R. L. TRITES, Principal Investigator
M. A. PRICE

This research project was funded under contract
by the Ministry of Education, Ontario

© The Minister of Education, Ontario, 1976
Queen's Park
Toronto, Ontario

MINISTRY OF EDUCATION, ONTARIO
COMMUNICATION SERVICES BRANCH
Printed by
13TH FLOOR, MOWAT BLOCK
TORONTO, ONTARIO M7A 1L3

The University of Ottawa Press

Additional copies may be ordered from:

The University of Ottawa Press
65 Hastey Avenue
Ottawa, Ontario
K1N 6N5

or

The Ontario Institute for Studies in Education
Publications Sales
252 Bloor Street West
Toronto, Ontario
M5S 1V6

or

Ontario Government Bookstore
880 Bay Street
Toronto, Ontario
M7A 1L2

ON 00101

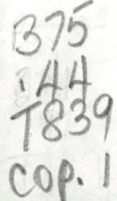

MINISTRY OF EDUCATION, ONTARIO
COMMUNICATION SERVICES BRANCH
13TH FLOOR, MOWAT BLOCK
TORONTO, ONTARIO M7A 1L3

ABSTRACT

Thirty-two children who experienced difficulty in primary French immersion were compared to seven other groups of children matched for age and sex on a wide variety of language, perceptual, academic achievement, memory, motor, sensory and other tests to determine if there was anything unique in the profile of this group. The comparison groups included three groups in which language is a factor; namely, English-speaking children in French language schools; French-speaking children in French language schools and children from other ethnic and language backgrounds in English language schools. The four "non-language" groups included standard diagnostic groups: hyperactive, minimal brain dysfunction, social and emotional maladjustment and primary reading disability. For further comparison purposes a group of eight children who were doing well in French immersion was included. Follow-up testing was obtained on twenty-four children who had difficulty in primary French immersion ("difficulty group") and seven children who were doing well in French immersion ("success group") for the purpose of monitoring their progress on academic achievement and language tests over time.

For data analysis, all of the children (N = 256) were pooled together. Using discriminant function statistics, the children were correctly classified in their proper groups at a significant level, indicating that there was something unique in the neuropsychological profile of the children who experienced difficulty in primary French immersion. The results point to a specific syndrome of sub-skill deficits in children who do poorly in this program in spite of above average intelligence. These are preliminary results and are currently being cross-validated. If this finding is replicated it points to a maturational lag in the temporal lobe regions of the brain which is a structure important in subserving language and auditory-perceptual functions.

Some other significant findings included the fact that a diagnosis of hyperactivity does not contra-indicate enrollment in primary French immersion, since some hyperactive children were doing well. However, there was some evidence that parental attitudes may be important. More parents of the French immersion "success group" attempted to speak French and they expressed a more integrative orientation to second language learning compared to the parents of the "difficulty group". However, the responses of the children to the instrumental-integrative questions were not different in the "success" and "difficulty" groups. Therefore, strong positive attitudes among the parents may contribute to the child's success.

Follow-up testing indicated that children who have difficulty in French immersion accelerated in academic skills after they had been switched to an English language program. However, at the time of the first follow-up they were still below expected levels considering their age and ability. The results of this study do not support the view that the child who had difficulty in primary French immersion would have experienced the same difficulty in an English language program. Rather, the findings support the conclusion that some children of above average potential and normal abilities for school progress in their native language experience difficulty or fail in a primary immersion program in a second language as a result of a mild specific maturational lag.

ACKNOWLEDGEMENTS

We would like to express our appreciation to Mr. H. Taylor, Computer Applications, Ottawa University, under whose auspices the extensive use of computer facilities was made possible; to Mr. Art Blouin, Ottawa University, who provided considerable assistance in some stages of the analysis; to Miss C. Fiedorowicz, Chief Technician, Neuropsychology Laboratory, who was helpful in screening subjects; and to Mr. Ken Johnson, Ottawa Valley Regional Office, Ministry of Education, Ontario, who offered continuous interest, support and encouragement throughout the project.

This research was made possible through the financial support of the Ministry of Education, Ontario, and their assistance is gratefully acknowledged.

TABLE OF CONTENTS

	page
INTRODUCTION.	1
1. Immersion Successes	1
2. Immersion Failures	5
3. Variables Affecting Second Language Learning	6
4. Second Language Learning and Reading	8
5. Variables Affecting Success in French Immersion Programs	10
BACKGROUND AND AIMS	12
THE SAMPLE.	14
1. French Immersion	14
2. Anglophones in Francophone Schools	16
3. Ethnic Groups in Anglophone Schools	17
4. Francophones in Francophone Schools	18
5. Reading Disability	19
6. Hyperactive	19
7. Behaviour and Personality Problems	20
8. Minimal Brain Dysfunction	20
9. French Immersion Success	21
10. Descriptive Data	22
11. Reasons for Referral	24
12. Diagnostic Impression	24
13. Transfer to the English Language Program from French Immersion	29
TESTS	31
ANALYSIS AND RESULTS.	35
1. Factor Analysis of the Neuropsychological Test Battery	35
2. Discriminant Function Analysis	38
3. One-Way Analyses of Variance	42
1) Intelligence Tests	46
2) Academic Achievement Tests	49
3) Auditory Perceptual Abilities	54
4) Motor and Sensory Tests	57
5) Tactual Performance Tests	60
6) Summary of the Eight Group Analysis	60
4. Two-Group Discriminant Function Analysis	63
5. Verbal IQ-Performance IQ Differences	73
FOLLOW-UP OF THE FRENCH IMMERSION SAMPLE.	77

		page
Amnestic, Attidudinal, Behavioural and Personality Data		78
1. Connors Parent's Questionnaire		78
a) Comparison of the Total French Immersion Difficulty Group and the French Immersion Success Group		78
b) Comparison of the Three French Immersion Difficulty Sub-groups and the French Immersion Success Group		81
2. Connors Teacher's Questionnaire		85
a) Comparison of the Total French Immersion Difficulty Group and the French Immersion Success Group		85
b) Comparison of the Three French Immersion Difficulty Sub-groups and the French Immersion Success Group		88
c) Connors' Ratings of the French Immersion-French Immersion Difficulty Group and the French Immersion Success Group by French Immersion and English Language Arts Teachers		90
3. Pupil Behaviour Rating Scale		90
a) Comparison of the Total French Immersion Difficulty Group and the French Immersion Success Group		90
b) Behaviour Ratings of the French Immersion-French Immersion Difficulty Group and the French Immersion Success Group by French Immersion and English Language Arts Teachers		92
4. Personality Testing		97
5. Amnestic and Attitudinal Information		97
a) Questions for Subject		97
i) Comparison of the Total French Immersion Difficulty Group and the French Immersion Success Group		97
ii) Comparison of the Three French Immersion Difficulty Sub-groups and the French Immersion Success Group		99
b) Family History of Reading Problems		101
i) Comparison of the Total French Immersion Difficulty Group and the French Immersion Success Group		100
ii) Comparison of the Three French Immersion Difficulty Sub-groups and the French Immersion Success Group		
c) Background Information		103
i) Comparison of the Total French Immersion Difficulty Group and the French Immersion Success Group		103

	page
ii) Comparison of the Three French Immersion Difficulty Groups and the French Immersion Success Group	107
iii) Comparison of the French Immersion Difficulty Children who have Remained in French Immersion versus the Two Groups of French Immersion Difficulty Children who have Switched to English	112

FOLLOW-UP ASSESSMENT: PSYCHOMETRIC AND ACADEMIC ACHIEVEMENT TESTS 115

ANALYSIS AND RESULTS 117
1. French Immersion Difficulty Group versus French Immersion Success Group 117

2. The Three French Immersion Difficulty Sub-groups versus the French Immersion Success Group 119
   a) Comparison of Difference Scores on the WISC Verbal IQ, WISC Performance IQ, Peabody IQ, and Wide Range Achievement Test 119
   b) Peabody Picture Vocabulary Test: Mental Age Scores and Receptive versus Reading Vocabulary 122
   c) Wide Range Achievement Test: Analysis of Discrepancy Scores 123
      i) Mean Discrepancy Scores 123
      ii) Discrepancy Score Frequencies 127
      iii) Discrepancy Scores: Difference Scores Between First and Second Testing 128
      iv) Test de Rendement en Français Results 130

DISCUSSION 131

1. Characteristics of Children who have Difficulty in French immersion . 133

2. Follow-up Testing 136
   a) Behavioural and Personality Data 136
   b) Questionnaire Responses 137
   c) Test Scores of the French immersion Difficulty Groups and the French immersion Success Group 138

3. Proposed Study for 1975-76 141

BIBLIOGRAPHY 143

Appendix
1. FRENCH IMMERSION PROGRAMS IN THE NATIONAL CAPITAL AREA 147

Appendix	page
2. QUESTIONNAIRES: FAMILY HISTORY OF READING PROBLEMS, CONNORS PARENT'S QUESTIONNAIRE, CONNORS TEACHER'S QUESTIONNAIRE, THE PUPIL RATING SCALE.	149
3. SPECIAL QUESTIONNAIRES: BACKGROUND INFORMATION AND QUESTIONS FOR SUBJECTS.	161
4. FACTOR LOADINGS OBTAINED FOR TESTS IN EACH OF THE FOUR FACTOR ANALYSES.	171
5. COMPARISON OF ALL SUBJECTS IN THE EIGHT GROUPS IN ONE-WAY ANOVAS AND NEWMAN-KEULS MULTIPLE COMPARISONS	175
6. COMPARISON OF THE EIGHT RESTRICTED AGE AND FSIQ SUB-SAMPLES IN ONE-WAY ANOVAS AND NEWMAN-KEULS MULTIPLE COMPARISONS.	179
7. PEABODY PICTURE VOCABULARY TEST DATA.	183
8. DISCREPANCY SCORES BETWEEN ACHIEVEMENT TEST SCORES AND BOTH ACTUAL AND EXPECTED GRADE LEVELS AT FIRST TESTING AND AT RETESTING FOR INDIVIDUAL SUBJECTS IN THE THREE FRENCH IMMERSION DIFFICULTY GROUPS AND THE FRENCH IMMERSION SUCCESS GROUPS	185
9. FREQUENCY AND PERCENT OF SUBJECTS IN EACH OF THE FOUR COMPARISON GROUPS SCORING BELOW AND AT OR ABOVE ACTUAL AND EXPECTED GRADE LEVELS ON THE WRAT.	189
10. INDIVIDUAL DIFFERENCE SCORES BETWEEN WRAT DISCREPANCY SCORES AT FIRST AND FOLLOW-UP TESTING FOR (A) ACTUAL GRADE LEVEL AND (B) EXPECTED GRADE LEVEL.	191

LIST OF TABLES

Table		page
I.-	Age, WISC FSIQ, Sex and Lateral Dominance of the Nine Groups	23
II.-	Reasons for Referral.	25
III.-	Diagnoses	26
IV.-	Reasons for Transfer from French Immersion to the English Program for the French Immersion Difficulty Group	30
V.-	Eigenvalue, Percentage of Variance Accounted for and Significance of the Discriminant Functions in the Eight Group Discriminant Function Analysis.	40
VI.-	Percent of Cases Correctly Classified in the Discriminant Function Analysis of the Eight Groups	41
VII.-	F-ratios for the Factors Comprising the Discriminant Functions in the Discriminant Function Analysis of Eight Groups	44
VIII.-	Summary of the Significant Differences Between the French Immersion Difficulty Group and Each of the Seven Comparison Groups Based on Newman-Keul's Test.	47
IX.-	Percent of Cases Correctly Classified in the Discriminant Function Analyses Involving Two Groups.	64
X.-	Discriminant Function Analysis: French Immersion Group (1) vs. Anglophones in Francophone Schools (2).	66
XI.-	Discriminant Function Analysis: French Immersion Group (1) vs. Ethnic Groups in Anglophone Schools (3)	67

Table	page
XII.- Discriminant Function Analysis: French Immersion Group (1) vs. Francophones in Francophone Schools (4)	68
XIII.- Discriminant Function Analysis: French Immersion Group (1) vs. Reading Disability (5)	70
XIV.- Discriminant Function Analysis: French Immersion Group (1) vs. Hyperactive (6)	71
XV.- Discriminant Function Analysis: French Immersion Group (1) Behaviour and Personality Problems (7)	72
XVI.- Discriminant Function Analysis: French Immersion (1) vs. Minimal Brain Dysfunction	74
XVII.- Mean Difference Scores (WISCPIQ-WISCVIQ) for the Eight Comparison Groups and the French Immersion Success Group	76
XVIII.- Mean Ratings, Standard Deviations and t-probabilities for the French Immersion Difficulty Group and the French Immersion Success Group on the Connors Parent's Questionnaire at First Testing and at Follow-up Testing	80
XIX.- Mean and Standard Deviation of Percent Scores on the Rating Scales of the Connors Parent's Questionnaire at Follow-up Testing	84
XX.- Mean and Standard Deviation of Percent Scores on the Rating Scales of the Connors Teacher's Questionnaire at Follow-up Testing	87
XXI.- Mean and Standard Deviation of Ratings of the French Immersion-French Immersion Difficulty Group and the French Immersion Success Group by French Immersion and English Language Arts Teachers	91

Table	page
XXII.- Mean, Standard Deviation and t-probabilities of Pupil Behaviour Ratings of the Total French Immersion Difficulty Group and the French Immersion Success Group at Follow-up Testing	93
XXIII.- Mean, Standard Deviation and t-probabilities of Pupil Behaviour Ratings by French Immersion and English Language Arts Teachers	95
XXIV.- Significant Findings for Comparisons Among the Three French Immersion Difficulty Sub-groups and the French Immersion Success Group on Questions for Subjects Questionnaire	100
XXV.- Significant Findings of the Chi^2 Analysis of the Family History of Reading Problems Questionnaire	102
XXVI.- Significant Findings in the Chi^2 Analysis of the Background Information Questionnaire comparing the Total French Immersion Difficulty Group and the French Immersion Success Group	105
XXVII.- Significant Findings in the Chi^2 Analysis of the Background Information Questionnaire for the Three French Immersion Difficulty Sub-groups and the French Immersion Success Group	109
XXVIII.- Significant Findings in the Chi^2 Analysis of the Background Information Questionnaire for the Comparison of the French Immersion-French immersion Difficulty Group and the Two Groups who have switched to English	113
XXIX.- Descriptive Information at Follow-up Testing	116

Table	page
XXX.- Mean, Standard Deviation and t-probability of Significant Differences Between the French Immersion Difficulty Group and the French Immersion Success Group at First Testing and at Follow-up Testing	118
XXXI.- Mean, Standard Deviation and Mean Difference Score and ANOVA Results for Selected Measures at First Testing and Retesting for the Four Comparison Groups	120
XXXII.- Mean WRAT Discrepancy Scores for Actual and Expected Grade Levels for All Subjects at First Testing	124
XXXIII.- Mean WRAT Discrepancy Scores at First and Second Testing for Actual and Expected Grade Levels for the Four Comparison Groups	126
XXXIV.- Mean Difference Scores for Actual and Expected Grade Level WRAT Discrepancy Scores for the Four Comparison Groups	129
1.- Appendix 7: Frequency and Percent of Various Chronological Age (CA) and Mental Age (MA) Relationships in the Four Comparison Groups.	184
2.- Appendix 7: Mean MA Scores at First Testing and Follow-up Testing and Differences Between these Means for the Four Comparison Groups.	184
3.- Appendix 7: Means for Peabody B-A at First Testing and Follow-up Testing for the Four Comparison Groups	184

LIST OF FIGURES

Figure   page

1.- Mean Scores Obtained by the Eight Comparison Groups on Various
    Intelligence Tests.   48

2.- Mean Scores Obtained by the Restricted Age and IQ Sub-sample
    on Various Intelligence Tests   50

3.- Mean Scores Obtained by the Eight Comparison Groups on the
    Wide Range Achievement Tests.   52

4.- Mean Scores Obtained by the Restricted Age and IQ Sub-sample
    on the Wide Range Achievement Tests   53

5.- Mean Scores Obtained by all Subjects in the Eight Comparison
    Groups and by the Age and IQ Restricted Sub-sample on Tests
    of Auditory Perceptual Abilities.   55

6.- Mean Scores Obtained by the Eight Comparison Groups on Certain
    Motor Tests   58

7.- Mean Scaled Scores Obtained on Certain Sensory and Motor Tests. .   59

8.- Mean Scores on the TPTOTT Measure for the Eight Comparison Groups
    and for the Restricted Age and IQ Sub-sample.   61

9.- Connors Parent's Symptom Questionnaire Ratings of the Total French
    Immersion Difficulty Group and the French Immersion Success
    Group at First Testing.   79

10.- Connors Parent's Symptom Questionnaire Ratings of the Total
     French Immersion Difficulty Group and the French Immersion
     Success Group at Follow-up Testing.   82

11.- Connors Parent's Symptom Questionnaire Ratings of the Three
     French Immersion Difficulty Groups and the French Immersion
     Success Group at Follow-up Testing.   83

Figure   page

12.- Connors Teacher's Symptom Questionnaire Ratings of the Total
     French Immersion Difficulty Group and the French Immersion
     Success Group at Follow-up Testing.   86

13.- Connors Teacher's Symptom Questionnaire Ratings of the Three
     French Immersion Difficulty Groups and the French Immersion
     Success Group at Follow-up Testing.   89

14.- Pupil Behaviour Ratings of the Total French Immersion Difficulty
     Groups and the French Immersion Success Group at Follow-up
     Testing   94

15.- Pupil Behaviour Ratings by French Immersion and English
     Language Arts Teachers.   96

16.- Early School Personality Questionnaire Profile of Twelve Subjects
     in the French Immersion Difficulty Group.   98

INTRODUCTION

As part of the transition in Canada towards greater English-French bilingualism, the school systems in several provinces extended their educational programs for teaching the French language. One such program is the early French immersion program in which English-speaking children beginning in the primary grades are exposed to French as the language of instruction for at least fifty percent of the school day. In most school systems, kindergarten and grade one are taught exclusively in French with instruction in the English language being introduced and gradually increased in later grades. Although some studies have outlined the favourable outcome of French immersion programming, little research has been concerned with children who have difficulty in such a program. It is with these children that this particular study was concerned.

At present, there is contradictory evidence regarding the success of early immersion programming as a means of acquiring proficiency in a second language without detrimental effects on native language skills. Studies describing a favourable outcome of immersion programming will be discussed below, followed by research outlining the negative aspects.

Immersion Successes

One study supporting a favourable outcome of immersion programming was conducted in the St. Lambert area of Montreal. Lambert and Tucker (1972) described the linguistic, intellectual and attitudinal development of English-speaking children in French immersion, followed from kindergarten through grade four compared to English-speaking children in regular English classes as well as French-speaking children in regular French classes. In general, the results of this investigation indicated that French immersion programming results in satisfactory proficiency in the French language for English-speaking children, without detrimental effects either to English language skills or to progress in other academic areas. However, the experimental nature of this program, as well as the possible selectivity of the children, (i.e. only the most capable children from an upper middle class area were in French immersion classes) along with the tremendous parental involvement and commitment to this program may have contributed to its substantial reported success.

Further investigations which followed the children in the St. Lambert French immersion program through grade five (Lambert, Tucker and D'Anglejan, 1973), grade six (Bruck, Lambert and Tucker, 1973), grade seven (Bruck, Lambert and Tucker, 1974) and through grade eight (Bruck, Lambert and Tucker, Undated) corroberated the success of French immersion programming. In addition, the results of a preliminary study of children from working class English-speaking homes who participated in a French immersion program in kindergarten and grade one, suggested that the program is also suitable for that sample of children (Tucker, Lambert and D'Anglejan, 1972). However, it is essential that they be followed at later grades and therefore, these preliminary findings should be viewed with caution.

Another group of studies, (Barik and Swain, 1973, 1975; Barik, McTavish and Swain, 1973, 1974) compared samples of children in French immersion classes and regular English classes on measures of intelligence, achievement in reading and arithmetic, and French comprehension. Attempts were made to follow the same, children from kindergarten, through grade three but, the samples differed at each grade level. Results indicated that French immersion programming did not have negative effects upon cognitive development. English language skills lagged slightly in grade one for French immersion children, but this was overcome in grade two, with the exception of spelling skills in some samples, after English Language Arts had been introduced. In the 1973-74 evaluation in the Ottawa area, French immersion children lagged in the development of English language skills at both the grade one and two levels but had also caught up to the English program sample by grade three (Barik and Swain, 1974a). These children also displayed adequate progress in arithmetic and in French comprehension. These results were interpreted as attesting to the general success of French immersion programming. However, children with hearing, perceptual or related problems were excluded from the testing and no information was provided regarding drop-outs from French immersion or children who did not do well.

Edwards and Casserly (1971, 1972, 1973) followed samples of children in French immersion programs as well as children in the English program who were instructed in French for 75-minutes per day, from grade one through grade three. These children were compared on measures of personality, achievement in arithmetic, language skills in English and French, visual, auditory and kinesthetic functioning, psycholinguistic abilities and intelligence. The children in French immersion did as well as the children in the English program in all areas, with the exception of a lag in English language skills in grade two which was overcome in grade three after the introduction of English Language Arts. The French immersion children showed greater progress in French as compared to the 75-minute group. Characteristics of children in these two programs were considered. Some personality differences were found and it was noted that children with intellectual, learning, language or environmental handicaps were encouraged to remain in the 75-minute program. In summary, results supported intensive second language training. However, the French immersion and 75-minute program samples differed in language and kindergarten background. The possibility that pre-selection factors favoured the French immersion sample was suggested.

In follow-up studies of early French immersion programming in Canada reported to date, several cautionary notes should be made. Of considerable importance there is clearly some degree of attrition in the number of children who continued in the French immersion program. Very rarely did these studies include a clear statement either to the number or percentage of children who drop out of the program, or to the reasons for dropping out of the program. In the St. Lambert area, 20 of the original 26 children in the pilot French immersion class were still in the program by grade five (Lambert, Tucker and D'Anglejan, 1973) and only 15 by grade seven (Bruck, Lambert and Tucker, 1973). Of the 38 children in the French immersion follow-up class, 30 were in the program by grade four (Lambert et al, 1973) and only 25 by grade six (Bruck et al, 1973). However, reasons for dropping out were not mentioned. Edwards and Casserly (1973) gave more details regarding drop-outs. Between grades one and two, there was a twenty percent decrease in enrollment. Between grades two and three, there was a sixteen percent decrease. The reasons cited for these drop out rates were vague, for example: 1) leaving the school system; 2) transferring to the English program or to the 75-minute French program because they were unable to handle immersion; 3) for transportation reasons.

In addition, the follow-up French immersion studies did not consider the children who had difficulty in French immersion programs. There was also a tendency towards selectivity in the choice of subjects. Edwards and Casserly (1973) suggested the possibility that pre-selection factors favoured the French immersion sample. Barik and Swain (1974) eliminated certain children from the analysis, such as "pupils who teachers indicated had special problems (e.g. serious hearing or vision difficulties, emotional problems); pupils who teachers indicated had a very limited ability to understand and express themselves in English." A study which has attempted to look at the progress of children in French immersion with special problems, namely learning disabilities (Bruck, Rabinovitch and Oates, 1975), will be discussed later.

Thus, there are clearly important unresolved questions regarding the outcome of the French immersion programs. The very favourable results reported may be based on very biased samples. Very little is known about the failures or of the children who experience difficulty in the immersion program. It is extremely important that efforts be made to define the characteristics of the marginally successful and failing students as well as the successful ones.

Immersion Failures

The above studies are quite unique in view of the fact that early immersion programming has not met with success in several countries. In Ireland, English-speaking children, for whom the language of instruction in school was Irish, did not achieve the same standard in written English as English monolinguals, or in written Irish as Irish monolinguals. The Irish immersion children also experienced retardation in problem-solving arithmetic but not in simple arithmetic computations (Macnamara, 1966).

Jones (1966) reported that English-speaking children taught in Welsh were below English monolinguals in English reading. A slight positive correlation was found between attitudes toward learning Welsh and Welsh achievements. Conversely if the parents' attitudes towards learning Welsh were negative, the children did poorly in this program.

In South Africa, it was observed that bilingual children taught in their mother tongue showed no adverse emotional reactions, but if children of lower intelligence were taught in the language with which they were less familiar, emotional disturbances could result (UNESCO Report, 1975).

Modiano (1968) found that children in Mexico whose native tongue was Tzeltal or Tzotzil, but who were given reading instruction in Spanish only, scored significantly lower on Spanish reading tests than the children who were taught to read in their native tongue first and later in Spanish.

In the United States, there has been much attention directed towards the progress of Spanish-speaking children attending English-speaking schools. In general, children in this English immersion program have not achieved competence in the English language comparable to that of English monolinguals and have had poor academic success (Macnamara, 1966; Gezi; 1974). In response to the failure of this immersion approach, bilingual education programs have been set up in which instruction begins in the vernacular moving gradually towards English. Improved academic success is observed among children in programs which offer instruction in their mother tongue (Gezi, 1974).

Variables Affecting Second Language Learning

There has been considerable interest in the variables affecting second language learning and the two factors most often cited as important determinants of success in second language learning are: (1) linguistic aptitude, and

2) attitudinal vairables (Barkman, 1969; Jones, 1966, Gardner and Lambert, 1959; Pimsleur, 1972; Stern, 1967, Mackey, 1967). Little is known about differences in language aptitude among children below age nine or ten; however, by these ages there is clear evidence that children vary in aptitude for foreign language learning (Carroll, 1969). Penfield's (1965) view that a child can best learn a second language before the age of 12 to 14 years, i.e. before the functional connections of the uncommitted cortex become fixed, has been used in support of early immersion. Others disagree that young children have greater capacity for learning a foreign language than adults and suggest that advantages of an early start are in the lack of self consciousness and longer period of study, rather than in the capacity of the learner (Carroll, 1969). The question of the optimal age to introduce a second language is still open to debate. In Canada, late French immersion programs at the grade eight and nine levels appear to be quite successful in advancing linguistic competence in French without persistent detrimental effects to English language skills or to subject matter taught in French (Barik and Swain, 1974b). As yet, however, early and late French immersion programs have not been compared systematically to determine their relative advantages and disadvantages.

Favourable attitudes towards the second language and the second language community facilitate second language learning (Mackey, 1967; Jones, 1966; Gardner and Smythe, 1973). High School students whose aim in second language learning is integrative, i.e. who wish to learn a second language in order to interact with, communicate with and to become a part of the second language community, are more successful in learning that language than students whose aims are utilitarian, or instrumental, for example, to increase employment opportunities (Gardner and Smythe, 1959; Lambert, 1974). In addition, the latter group tended to drop out of high school French courses more often (Gardner and Smythe, 1973). English-speaking children whose parents resented Welsh as the medium of instruction in the schools did poorly in immersion programming (Jones, 1966).

Sociological factors, such as the relative prestige of the first and second languages (Paulsten, 1974) as well as perceptions and beliefs about the other ethnolinguistic group (Lambert, 1974) have been cited as possible factors affecting the contradictory findings regarding the success of early immersion programs.

Second Language Learning and Reading

Controversy exists over the advisability of introducing reading in a child's second language before he learns to read in his mother tongue. Downing (Undated) has suggested that language mismatch between home and school language causes retardation in the development of reading skills. Studies cited earlier pointed to the retardation of reading skills in both the first and second language when the child was taught to read initially in a second language (Macnamara, 1966), to the retardation in native language reading skills when initial reading was taught in a second language (Jones, 1966), and to improved reading ability in a second language when the child was taught to read initially in the vernacular (Modiano, 1968). Miller (1973) also pointed out the importance of the match of home and school environments for success in reading. Gezi (1974) reviewed studies of bilingual and bicultural education and stressed the importance of the mother tongue as a medium of instruction.

In contrast, studies of the reading skills of children in French immersion in Canada indicated that reading levels in French were below those of French monolinguals but that any retardation in English language skills is overcome with the introduction of formal English reading instruction. Swain (1974) has suggested that it is easier to rea in French than in English becuase the former has a more systematic sound-symbol correspondence. The basics of reading are then easily transferred because the vocabulary and language structures are already established. However, contradictory findings regarding reading achievement in English arise when one compares children in partial French immersion programs who are taught to read in English initially and children in total French immersion programs who are taught to read in French initially. Swain (1974) reported that one group of children in a partial French immersion program (in St. Thomas School) were better readers in English in grades one, two and three than children in a total French immersion program who had not had any English Language Arts instruction; however, grade two or three children in a total French immersion program who had received one year of English Language Arts instruction could read as well in English as children in the same grade in a partial French immersion program. Both immersion groups had poorer English reading test scores than grade two and three children in the regular English program. Thus in this sample, learning to read in the vernacular did not appear to enhance reading skills. In contrast, another group of children in a partial French immersion program who were taught to read initially in English did appear to have enhanced reading skills in English. Children in a grade three partial immersion class at Rosyln school were better readers in English than children in a total French immersion program regardless of the grade in which English Language Arts were introduced. With regard to reading skills in French, being taught to read initially in French appears to promote better reading skills in French, since children in total French immersion outperformed children in partial French immersion on French reading tests. However, when comparisons were made on the basis of amount of exposure to French, partial immersion programs appeared to produce levels of proficiency in reading French comparable to the reading levels achieved by children in total French immersion programs. Both immersion groups were poorer readers in French than French monolinguals.

Tucker (1974) reported that for pupils in grade one and grade two French immersion programs, reading achievement in French was a good predictor of reading achievement in English at each grade level and he stressed the apparently easy transfer of reading skills from French to English. However, in view of contradictory evidence, further investigation of this problem is needed and, as yet, no definitive statement can be made regarding the optimal sequencing of initial reading instruction in bilingual educational programs.

Variables Affecting Success in French Immersion Programs

A few studies have considered specific descriptive or test variables as they relate to performance in French immersion programs. Dockrell and Brosseau (1967) investigated the relationship of chronological age, mental age and attitude to three measures of French achievement (vocabulary size, pronunciation and comprehension) among 40 children in French immersion kindergarten. Older subjects showed greater improvement in vocabulary size and comprehension and less improvement in pronunciation. Attitude measured in an interview was related to all aspects of French achievement, while an attitude questionnaire was related only to vocabulary size. General intelligence was correlated with vocabulary only, and not comprehension or pronunciation. This correlational analysis did not give a clear picture of factors affecting second language learning or the underlining complexity of such relationships.

Alexander, Hallows and Tiltens (1974) gave measures of reading achievement, perception, intelligence and emotional development to 18 grade two pupils who had dropped out of French immersion, and to 18 grade two pupils who remained in French immersion. No differences were found on intelligence or perceptual measures, while the second group performed better in reading. The "drop-outs" were more assertive and tense. There were many problems with this study including a failure to match subjects on several measures.

With respect to children with learning disabilities, a study in Montreal (Bruck, Rabinovitch and Oates, 1975) focused on the effects of French immersion programs on children with language disabilities. The investigators concluded that the children fare well, in that they learn to read in both English and French. They also concluded that first language acquisition did not appear to have been retarded by the placement in a French immersion program. However, there were several difficulties with this study. The most serious difficulty was that, as the authors state, the conclusions were based on an extremely small sample of subjects, basically a sample of three to six children depending upon the date of follow-up. Most serious, however, is the fact that several of the group means on the various tests appeared to be spurious and misleading. For example, French immersion learning disability children were reported by grade two to be reading and spelling in English at the 1.9 and 2.2 levels respectively, and the French immersion control group obtained grade equivalent scores of reading 5.9 and spelling 5.2 which, in both instances, opened a serious question, particularly, since the French control group appeared to be about two years in advance of an English control group and an English learning disability group. Indications of other probable serious sampling errors were seen in the fact that for some peculiar reason, at several grade levels, the English problem children appeared to be reading better than their controls and both groups were only slightly ahead of the French immersion problem group. Any conclusions based on this study must be held in abeyance until more adequate studies employing larger samples and more stringent control groups and also using more exhaustive diagnostic testing have been conducted.

BACKGROUND AND AIMS

One of the functions of the Neuropsychology Laboratory at the Royal Ottawa Hospital, in operation since late 1969, is to perform a detailed examination of children with learning disabilities. Children referred to the laboratory, are given a six to eight hour examination on tests which have also been standardized in Ottawa in French and English. The test battery is designed to determine the type of learning disability the child may have and to help in determining the cause for the disability. The test battery, described more fully below, includes a variety of tests of psychometric ability, academic achievement reasoning skills, language development, auditory perceptual functions, visual motor functions, motor and sensory tests, as well as personality screening devices. Over 2,000 children from the Ottawa region have been assessed on this extensive battery of tests, many for three or four retests.

The French immersion program began in the Ottawa Schools in 1969 and 1970 with programs at the kindergarten level. These are described in Appendix 1. It had become apparent by 1973 that increasing numbers of children from French immersion programs were being referred to the Neuropsychology Laboratory for examination. Most of the children had important deficiencies in their school progress in spite of at least normal intelligence, and no evidence of brain dysfunction. Also, in general, these children could not readily be classified as having dyslexia, other types of perceptual or learning disabilities or "minimal cerebral dysfunction". It was considered possible, that if these children were in an English language program, their progress through school might have been uneventful. An attempt was made by surveying the literature to see what factors were correlated with poor progress in immersion programs. It was clear that there are no guidelines whatsoever for attempting to identify high risk children.

The purpose of this preliminary and descriptive study was to identify a group of children who are described by their teachers and parents, as having difficulty in their French immersion programs. The aim of this study was to see if these children resembled in any consistent way, other groups of children who had difficulty in school progress. A total of seven control groups were composed. Three control groups had a language factor in their learning difficulty. One of these control groups included children from English language backgrounds, who were enrolled in a French-speaking school. A French school in the Ottawa area differs from a French immersion program in that, not only is the language of instruction in the classroom French, but the classmates are essentially native French-speaking children and French is generally the language of communication outside of the classroom. A second language control group included children from other ethnic backgrounds (Italian, Greek, etc.) who attended English language schools. A third language control group included children from French-speaking homes who attended a French language school. For further comparison, other clinical groups of children were composed: a) children who are diagnosed as having a primary reading disability (dyslexia); b) children who are hyperactive; c) children who are diagnosed as having behavioural or personality adjustment problems; d) children who are classified as having "minimal cerebral dysfunction". These "non-language" comparison groups were included to see if children who have difficulty in a French immersion program resemble, in important ways, children who might have been expected to have difficulty in any event. For example, if it turned out that the profiles of the French immersion difficulty group and the dyslexic group were extremely similar, then it could be concluded that these children would likely have had difficulty in any event, particularly insofar as the development of reading and spelling skills is concerned. An additional but smaller group of children who were considered to be doing well in their French immersion program was also identified and used for further comparison purposes. Many of the children in the French immersion group were brought in for follow-up testing to assess their progress on selected measures including academic achievement tests. Various questionnaires and demographic forms were also completed at that time.

THE SAMPLE

A total of 264 subjects were selected for study and 31 were brought in for follow-up testing. The subjects were chosen from among children tested in the Neuropsychology Laboratory between March of 1970 and March of 1975. Eight groups, each composed of 32 subjects, were formed on the basis of the following criteria. A ninth group was composed of eight subjects who were not having difficulty in French immersion.

1) <u>French immersion</u>

Home language: English

School language: English

Classroom language: At least 50% French at kindergarten but 100% French in grade one, and 80% to 100% in grade two.

Problem: The child is experiencing, or has experienced at some time, difficulty in French immersion. Information from parent and teacher reports and achievement testing was used to decide whether or not the child was having difficulty. The difficulty may have been strictly in learning or also involved problems in adjusting to the French immersion program.

Home language(s):	English	32
	Some French	7
Language of testing:	English	32
School language:	French class (English school) at testing	22
	English class (English school) at testing	10

Length of time in school:

In French immersion	Mean	14.8 months
	Range	1 to 42 months
In English program since transfer	Mean	10.3 months
	Range	1 to 29 months
Special Education:	In English	2
Repeated grades/Remedial help:	Total	10
	In French immersion	7
	In English program	3

Reasons for transfer to English program:	Learning difficulty	5
	Behaviour Problem	2
	Emotional Reaction	3
School Boards Represented:	Ottawa Separate	4
	Carleton Separate	3
	Ottawa	14
	Carleton	11

After 32 subjects were classified in the French immersion group, 32 subjects were selected to compose the following seven groups. They were matched as closely as possible to the French immersion subjects in terms of age and sex.

2) **Anglophones in francophone schools**

Home language: English
School language: French
Classroom language: French
Problem: The child is experiencing, or has experienced difficulty in a French school. Again, parent and teacher reports and achievement testing were used to decide whether or not the child was having difficulty in the French school.

Home language(s):	English	32
	English, some french	9
Language of testing:	English	32
School language:	French at testing	17
	English at testing (previously French)	15

Length of time in school:

French schools	Mean	25.3 months
	Range	3 to 66 months
English schools	Mean	13.5 months
since transfer	Range	1 to 31 months

Special Education:

Total	3
In French school	1
In English school	1
In both schools	1

Repeated grades/Remedial help:

Total	9
In French school	1
In English school	6
In both schools	2

3) Ethnic groups in anglophone schools

Home language: Other than English

School language: English

Classroom language: English

Problem: Having difficulty in school.

Home language(s):

German	10
Italian	7
French	3
Dutch	2
Polish	2
Arabic	1
Chinese	1

	Greek	1
	Hungarian	1
	Islamic	1
	Spanish	1
	Tagalog	1
	Turkish	1
Language of testing:	English	32
School language:	English	32
Length of time in school:	Mean	28.3 months
	Range	7 to 56 months
Special Education:		7
Repeated grades/Remedial help:		9

4) **Francophones in francophone schools**

Home language: French

School language: French

Classroom language: French

Problem: Having difficulty in school.

Home language(s):	French	32
	Some English	12
Language of testing:	English	8
	French	24
School language:	French	32
Length of time in school:	Mean	29.4 months
	Range	5 to 50 months

Special Education: 8

Repeated grades/Remedial help: 2

5) Reading disability

Home language: English

School language: English

Classroom language: English

Problem: Difficulty in school, especially reading and diagnosed as a
                    primary reading disability or specific language retardation.

Home language(s):	English	32
Language of testing:	English	32
School language:	English	32
Length of time in school:	Mean	31.7 months
	Range	11 to 54 months

Special Education: 8

Repeated grades/Remedial help: 19

6) Hyperactive

Home language: English

School language: English

Classroom language: English

Problem: Child who is diagnosed as hyperactive and who is having
                    difficulty in school.

Home language(s):	English	32
Language of testing:	English	32
School language:	English	32

Length of time in school:	Mean	21.9 months
	Range	2 to 41 months
Special Education:		6
Repeated grades/Remedial help:		13

7) **Behaviour and personality problems**

Home language: English

School language: English

Classroom language: English

Problem: Children who have behaviour or personality adjustment problems and who are having difficulty in school.

Home language(s):	English	32
Language of testing:	English	32
School language:	English	32
Length of time in school:	Mean	26.7 months
	Range	6 to 51 months
Special Education:		11
Repeated grades/Remedial help:		8

8) **Minimal brain dysfunction**

Home language: English

School language: English

Classroom language: English

Problem: Children who are having difficulty in school and whose tests show evidence of cerebral dysfunction.

Home language(s):	English	32

Language of testing:	English	32
School language:	English	32
Length of time in school:	Mean	26.7 months
	Range	3 to 60 months
Special Education:		6
Repeated grades/Remedial help:		7

9) French immersion success

A ninth group composed of eight subjects who were doing well in the French immersion program were included in the data analysis for comparison purposes.

Home language: English
School language: English
Classroom language: French
Problem: Children referred for a variety of problems but who are not experiencing difficulty in the French immersion program.

Home language(s):	English	8
	Some French	3
Language of testing:	English	8
School language:	English	8
Length of time in school		
In French immersion:	Mean	22 months
	Range	2 to 46 months
Special Education:	None	
Repeated grades/Remedial help:	None	

Descriptive Data

The means and standard deviations of age and Full Scale IQ based on the Wechsler Intelligence Scale for Children (WISC FSIQ) are presented in Table I.

Insert Table I About Here

This table also contains t-probalities for t-test comparisons of the French immersion group with each of the eight comparison groups on the above variables. Sex and lateral dominance are also presented in Table I. It can be seen from Table I that with respect to the comparison between the French immersion group and all other groups, the French immersion group are significantly younger in age from all groups except the hyperactive, minimal brain dysfunction and French immersion success groups. It would appear that children who have difficulty in French immersion, perhaps because of the novelty of the program, are identified and referred for assessment at a very early age. The same holds true with the hyperactive children, probably as a result of the disruption that they cause in the classroom.

The French immersion group had a higher WISC FSIQ than the three language comparison groups (anglophones in francophone schools, ethnic groups in anglophone schools and francophones in francophone schools) as well as the minimal brain dysfunction group. Thus, this was a bright young group of children.

It is of interest that there was a high percentage of females in the French immersion group. Most surveys of learning disabilities of one sort or another report a very high ratio, generally three, four and even five to one of males to

TABLE I

Age, WISC FSIQ, Sex and Lateral Dominance of the Nine Groups

GROUPS	AGE Mean	AGE S.D.	AGE t-prob.[1]	WISC FSIQ Mean	WISC FSIQ S.D.	WISC FSIQ t-prob.	SEX Males	SEX Females	DOMINANCE Left	DOMINANCE Right
French immersion	7.0	1.2		104.3	10.6		22	10	9	23
Anglophones in francophone schools	8.2	1.7	0.002**	97.7	12.5	0.028*	26	6	8	24
Ethnic groups in anglophone schools	8.0	1.5	0.007**	95.3	13.7	0.005**	24	8	1	31
Francophones in francophone schools	8.4	1.1	0.000**	94.0	10.7	0.000**	27	5	2	30
Reading disability	8.3	1.0	0.000**	104.8	8.5	0.836	22	10	10	22
Hyperactive	7.2	1.7	0.533	101.3	9.7	0.244	30	2	5	27
Behaviour and personality problems	7.8	1.1	0.019*	101.8	11.5	0.373	24	8	5	27
Minimal brain dysfunction	7.8	1.6	0.058	96.9	10.2	0.006**	21	11	9	23
French immersion success	7.1	1.8	0.947	103.1	15.1	0.843	6	2	1	7

[1] The t-tests referred to involve the comparison of the French immersion group with each of the eight comparison groups.

*p<.05
**p<.01

females, whereas the ratio was two males to one female in the French immersion group. For this reason, it was very difficult to make sex matches in some of the control groups even though there were 2,000 cases to choose from. Handedness was not controlled in the matching and the French immersion group had significantly more left handers than ethnic groups in anglophone schools and francophones in francophone schools.

Reasons for Referral

As can be seen from Table II the two most frequent reasons for referral

---

Insert Table II About Here

---

were difficulty in school and behaviour problems, with the exception of the reading problem frequently reported in the reading disability group. The reasons for referral are quite similar in the French immersion group as compared to most other groups. None of the children in the French immersion success group were referred for difficulty in school.

Diagnostic Impression

The diagnosis given following the Neuropsychological examination is presented in Table III. The total diagnosis for any one group exceeds 32 since up to

---

Insert Table III About Here

---

three diagnoses can be given for each subject, for example reading disability plus epilepsy plus hereditary. It is of interest to look at the French immersion group

TABLE II

Reasons for Referral

	French immersion	Anglophones in francophone schools	Ethnic groups in anglophone schools	Francophones in francophone schools	Reading disability	Hyperactive	Behaviour and personality problems	Minimal brain dysfunction	French immersion success.[1]
Difficulty in school	17	18	11	16	14	10	9	8	
Difficulty in school plus behaviour problems	3	8	13	6	1	3	10	6	
Difficulty in school plus speech problems		1	2	2				1	
Difficulty in school plus motor problems	1	1	1	2				2	
Difficulty in school plus medical problems	1	1	5	2	3			4	
Reading problem	3	2		3	14	4	2	1	
Behaviour problem	7	1				15	10		1
Head injury/Medical problem				1			1	1	1
Hyperactivity								10	4

[1]. One subject in this group was referred because his brother had a reading problem and another for difficulty in expressing himself.

TABLE III

Diagnoses

	French immersion Diagnosis #				Anglophones in francophone schools Diagnosis #				Ethnic groups in anglophone schools Diagnosis #			
	1	2	3	Total	1	2	3	Total	1	2	3	Total
Difficulty in school	12	6	2	20	13	6	1	20	7	7	1	15
Specific language, perceptual or motor retardation	4	3	1	8	5	2		7	7	2	2	11
Hyperactivity	6	3	1	10	3	5		8	7	5		12
Primary reading disabilities	2	1		3	2	1		3				
Psychopathology; No brain damage	1	1		2	2	3		5	2			2
Hereditary and Congenital		1		1	2			2	0			
Perinatal	3	0	1	4	1	2		3	2			2
Brain damage neither proven nor ruled out		2		2	1	2	1	4	1		1	2
Miscellaneous diseases; no brain damage	1	0	1									
Head injuries	2	0		2	1			1	4			4
Infectious	1	0		1					0			1
Seizures		1		1					2	1		3
Drug Use					1			1				
Miscellaneous brain conditions										1		1

TABLE III (cont'd.)

	Francophones in francophone schools Diagnosis #				Reading Disability Diagnosis #				Hyperactive Diagnosis #			
	1	2	3	Total	1	2	3	Total	1	2	3	Total
Difficulty in school	7	5	2	14	4	2		6	1	13	3	17
Specific language, perceptual or motor retardation	4	2		6	8	2		10	1	4	1	6
Hyperactivity	7	1		8		1		1	28	3		31
Primary reading disabilities	2	1		3	19	2		21				
Psychopathology; No brain damage	2	2		4						1		1
Hereditary and Congenital	3			3		1		1				
Perinatal						1		1	1			1
Brain damage neither proven nor ruled out	3	3		6		2		2		1		1
Miscellaneous diseases; no brain damage										1		1
Head injuries	3			3	1	1		2	1			1
Infectious												
Seizures	1	1		2								
Drug Use												
Miscellaneous brain conditions												

TABLE III (cont'd.)

	Behaviour and personality problems Diagnosis #				Minimal brain dysfunction Diagnosis #				French immersion success Diagnosis #			
	1	2	3	Total	1	2	3	Total	1	2	3	Total
Difficulty in school	9	7		16	5	4	4	13			4	4
Specific language, perceptual or motor retardation	1			1	1	1	3	5		1	3	4
Hyperactivity	4			4		2		2	5	2		7
Primary reading disabilities												
Psychopathology; No brain damage	3			3								
Hereditary and Congenital					2	1		3				
Perinatal					2	2		4	1			1
Brain damage neither proven nor ruled out	1			1	1	2		3				
Miscellaneous diseases; no brain damage												
Head injuries	1	1		2	7			7	1			1
Infectious					4			4				
Seizures					6	5		11	1			1
Drug Use	1			1								
Miscellaneous brain conditions	1	1		2	4	2	1	7			1	1

and see that only three were diagnosed as having a primary reading disability, less than one third were diagnosed as hyperactive and even fewer as having specific language, perceptual or motor retardation. There was a similar lack of specific group membership in the three language control groups. This finding is of considerable interest since the particular aim of this investigation was to see if children who have difficulty in French immersion are in fact children who can be classified into standard learning disability categories such as perceptual disorder or reading disability. This finding would suggest that they cannot and thus other factors may be operating here.

Transfer to the English Language Program from French Immersion

Of the 32 children in the French immersion difficulty group, 17 were transferred to an English language program, ten at the time of first testing and an additional seven before follow-up testing. Twelve, or 70.6%, were transferred before grade two, and five, or 29.4%, were transferred in grade two or three. The reasons for transfer are presented in Table IV. In the total group of transfers, the

---

Insert Table IV About Here

---

reason for transfer can be summarized as follows:

Reason for Transfer	Primary	Secondary	Total
1) Learning difficulty	52.9%	23.5%	76.5%
2) Behaviour problem	23.5%	11.8%	35.3%
3) Emotional reaction	17.6%	5.9%	22.5%
4) No program available	5.9%		5.9%

TABLE IV

Reasons for Transfer from French Immersion to the English Program for the French Immersion Difficulty Group

| Grade Level | Reasons for Transfer to English ||||| Primary Reasons ||
	Learning Difficulty	Behaviour Problem	Emotional Reaction	No program available	Total	Percent
During Kindergarten	1[1]	1	2		3	17.6
After Kindergarten	2	1		1	3	17.6
During Grade 1	1,2	2	1		4	23.5
After Grade 1	2				2	11.8
During Grade 2	1				1	5.9
After Grade 2	3		1		3	17.6
During Grade 3	1	1			1	5.9
Total	9,4	4,1	3,1	1	17	
Percent Total	76.5%	35.3%	47.6%	11.8%		
Primary	52.9	23.5	17.6	5.9		
Secondary	23.5	11.8	5.9			

1. Secondary reasons for transfer are underlined. Other numbers refer to the frequency of primary reasons.

Broken down by grade and age, the reasons for transfers can be summarized as follows:

	Transfers before Grade 2 (12 subjects)			Transfers Grade 2 & 3 (5 subjects)		
	Primary	Secondary	Total	Primary	Secondary	Total
1)	41.7%	25%	66.7%	80%	20%	100%
2)	25	16.7	41.7	20		20
3)	25	2	25		20	20
4)	8.3		8.3			0

Although learning difficulty was the most frequent reason for transfer to English programs at the lower and higher grade levels, it was important in 100% of the cases in grades two and three, but only 66.7% at the lower grades. Behaviour problems were about the same at the two levels but at the older level, "emotional reactions" became secondary. At the younger levels, parents and teachers may be quite concerned about the child's happiness and adjustment in the program, while at the older age levels it seems that learning difficulties become the sole focus of attention.

TESTS

Extensive history information was obtained on each of the 264 children in the study which included birth history, developmental milestones, medical and neurological history (including exact records where applicable such as EEG recordings, details of drug use such as Ritalin, etc.), social and emotional development, family relations and school performance. This information in each case was obtained from parents, school authorities, social agencies and physicians. In addition, each child received an extensive six to eight hour neuropsychological examination which included:

                                                                    Computer Code

1. Psychometric Tests

    Wechsler Intelligence Scale for Children   WISCVIQ
    (Verbal IQ, Performance IQ, Full Scale IQ)   WISCPIQ
                                                                    WISCFSIQ

    Raven Progressive Matrices Test   MATRST
    (non-verbal measure of ability)

    Peabody Picture Vocabulary Test   PEABBA
    (receptive vocabulary ability as well as   PEABIQ
     reading vocabulary ability)

2. Adaptive Abilities
    (Halstead-Reitan Tests of biological intelligence)

    Category Test   CATOTT
    (non-verbal abstraction-concept formation)

    Tactual Performance Test   TPTOTT
    (psychomotor problem-solving ability,   TPTLOCT
     memory component, spatial-location component)   TPTMEMT

    Finger tapping rates   FINTAPDT
    (speed of finger movements of the dominant   FINTAPNT
     and non-dominant hands)

    Boston Speech Perception   BOSTONT
    (auditory perception)

3. Motor Skills

    Fine Manipulative Skills   PEGDT
    (a measure of dexterity of the fingers)   PEGNT
                                                                    PEGDNT
                                                                    PEGNNT

    Steadiness   STEADDTT
    (a measure of resting tremor)   STEADNTT
                                                                    STEADDCT
                                                                    STEADNCT

    Maze Steadiness and Movement   MAZEDTTT
     Co-ordination   MAZENTTT
    (a measure of gross motor coordination)   MAZEDCT
                                                                    MAZENCT

	Computer Code
Foot tapping rates (speed of foot movement of the dominant foot and non-dominant foot)	FOOTAPDT FOOTAPNT
Vertical Groove (a measure of movement steadiness)	VERGDTTT VERGNTTT VERGDCT VERGNCT

4. Sensory Examination

Finger Agnosia (ability to localize tactual stimulation to the fingers)	FINGAGDT FINGAGNT
Tactile Form Recognition (ability to recognize geometric forms placed in the hand-stereognosis)	TACTFDT TACTFNT TACTFDET TACTFNET

5. Miscellaneous Tests

Frostig Visual Perceptual Battery (a variety of eye-hand co-ordination and visual perceptual tasks)	PERCQUOT
Illinois Test of Psycholinguistic abilities (a variety of tests of language functions)	MCANSCAL

Tests of attention span and concentration ability
  Visual attention span (Knox Cube Test)
  Auditory attention span (WISC subtest)
  Tactile memory (Tactual Performance Test)
	
	KNOXMEMQ
	WISCDSP
	TPTMEMT

Right-Left Discrimination (Twelve items measuring right-left orientation ability)	RLDISCT
Lateral Dominance Test (Includes measures of preference for hand, eye and foot.)	LATDOM(HR)(HL) (ER)(EL)(FR)(FL) (DR)(DL)(AR)(AL)
Developmental Drawings Test (ability to reproduce geometric drawings)	DEVDRAWT

6. Academic Achievement Testing
   (reading, spelling and arithmetic grade levels)

WRARSS
WRASSS
WRAASS

                                                                Computer Code

7. Personality and Social Skills

   Early School Personality Questionnaire   ESPQ
   (an objective measure of personality)

   Vineland Social Maturity Scale   VINELAND
   (a questionnaire responded to by the parents on
   which they rate the child's level of development of
   social and self-help skills)

   Myklebust Pupil Rating Scale   AUDCOMP
   (see Appendix 2)   SPOKLANG
                                                               ORIENT
                                                               MOTCORD
                                                               PERSOC
                                                               VERB
                                                               NONVER
                                                               TOTAL

   Connors Teacher's Questionnaire   TPROB
   (see Appendix 2)   TPASS
                                                               TANX
                                                               THYPER
                                                               TEACHTOT

   Connors Parent's Questionnaire   PPROB
   (see Appendix 2)   PANX
                                                               PHYP
                                                               PLEARN
                                                               PPSYSOM
                                                               PPERF
                                                               PANTSOC
                                                               PTENSE
                                                               PARENTOT

Certain of the children in the French immersion difficulty group and in the French immersion success group were brought in for retesting on selected measures. The retest battery consisted of:

   Wechsler Intelligence Scale for Children
   Peabody Picture Vocabulary Test
   Wide Range Achievement Test
   Connors Rating Scale for Parents (Appendix 2)
   Connors Rating Scale for Teachers (Appendix 2)

Test de Rendement en Francais (1973-74)
Family History of Reading Disability (Appendix 2)
Specially Designed Questionnaire for Children
and Parents in this French immersion study (Appendix 3)

ANALYSIS AND RESULTS

Factor Analysis of the Neuropsychological Test Battery

The data on each of the subjects were coded and stored on magnetic tape for the purpose of computer analysis.

The neuropsychological test battery contains various motor and sensory tests for which there are important developmental factors to consider in assessing age changes. Age differences were controlled by calculating T-scores for tests which did not have built in scales permitting comparison across age levels. The T-scores were calculated using age norms developed in the Neuropsychology Laboratory on over 2,000 children. Therefore, they are not norms of the general population, but norms of a population of children referred to the laboratory for assessment for a variety of reasons.

The neuropsychological test battery, along with all the other measures used in this study, yielded a very large number of dependent variables which were used for between group discrimination. A useful statistical procedure has been applied in this Laboratory employing factor analytic techniques for data reduction purposes. Based on logical assumptions about measurement dimensions, the tests can be divided into groups. Logical considerations determine the test groupings available. We have found in previous studies, however, that altering test groupings has only minimal effects on the configuration of factors.

Each group of tests were factor analyzed using the sample of 256 subjects, excluding the small French immersion success group. From each factor analysis, two to five interpretable factors were determined. The SPSS SUB-PROGRAM FACTOR (Nie, Hull, Jenkins, Steinbrenner and Bent, 1975) calculates factor scores from the factor score coefficient matrix. The factor scores were retained on a raw-output-data-file. The large number of original dependent variables from the test battery were, thus, reduced to a small set of factor scores. The factor scores were used as new dependent variables in a discriminant function analysis.

The neuropsychological tests were divided into the following four groups and four independent factor analyses were performed. The factor loadings for tests in each of these analyses are presented in Appendix 4.

1. Tests of General Intelligence and Academic Achievement were selected and they include the following: WISCVIQ, WISCPIQ, PEABBA, PEABIQ, VINELAND, WRARSS, WRASSS, WRAASS, MATRST, DEVDRAWT, CATOTT.

A factor analysis of these measures yielded three easily interpretable factors as follows:

A̲ A Performance Intelligence Factor - PRFINTOT, which included the following variables with the highest loadings: WISCPIQ, MATRST, DEVDRAWT, CATOTT.

B̲ An Academic Achievement Factor - ACADTOT, which included the following variables with the highest loadings: WRASSS, WRARSS, WRAASS.

C̲ A Verbal Intelligence Factor - VRBINTOT, which included the following variables with the highest loadings: WISCVIQ, PEABIQ.

2. The perceptual tests from the neuropsychological battery were selected for a factor analysis and they included the following variables: PERCQUOT, MCANSCAL, BOSTONT, KNOXMEMQ, RLDISCT. The factor analysis yielded two factors:

<u>A</u> An Auditory Perceptual Factor - PERCTOTA on which the two following variables had the highest loadings: MCANSCAL and BOSTONT.

<u>B</u> A Visual Perceptual Factor - PERCTOTB, which included the following variables with the highest loadings: PERCQUOT and KNOXMEMQ.

3.   Certain of the lateral dominance scores and the accuracy scores from tests of movement co-ordination and resting steadiness were included together for the third factor analysis. These variables specifically included: LATDOMHL, LATDOMEL, LATDOMFL, LATDOMAL, LATDOMNL, MAZEDCT, MAZENCT, VERGDCT, VERGNCT, STEADDCT, STEADNCT. This factor analysis yielded four factors.

<u>A</u> A Resting Steadiness Measure - STEADCT, which included the following two measures with the highest loadings: STEADDCT and STEADNCT.

<u>B</u> A Vertical Movement Accuracy Measure - VERGCT, which included the following two variables with the highest loadings: VERGDCT and VERGNCT.

<u>C</u> A Maze Co-ordination Accuracy Measure - MAZECT, which included the following two variables with the highest loadings: MAZEDCT and MAZENCT.

<u>D</u> Lateral Preference Measure - LATDOMLM, which included the following three variables with the highest loadings: LATDOMHL, LATDOMFL and LATDOMEL.

4.   The fourth factor analysis was performed on various sensory tests and tests of motor movement. The following variables were included: LATDOMHR, LATDOMER, LATDOMFR, LATDOMAR, LATDOMNR, TPTOTT, TPTMEMT, TPTLOCT, FINGTAPDT, FINGTAPNT, FOOTAPDT, FOOTAPNT, MAZEDTTT, MAZENTTT, VERGDTTT, VERGNTTT, TACTFDT, TACTFNT, TACTFDET, TACTFNET, STEADDTT, STEADNTT, PEGDT, PEGNT, PEGDNT, PEGNNT, FINGAGDT, FINGAGNT.

This factor analysis yielded five factors:

<u>A</u> VERGMOT - which included the following variables with the highest loadings: VERGDTTT and VERGNTTT.

<u>B</u> STMAZMOT - which included the following variables with the highest loadings: STEADDTT and STEADNTT.

<u>C</u> TAPMOT - which included the following variables with the highest loadings: FINTAPDT, FINTAPNT, FOOTAPDT, FOOTAPNT.

<u>D</u> PGTACTPT - which included the following variables with the highest loadings: TPTOTT, TPTMEMT, TPTLOCT, TACTFDT, TACTFNT, TACTFDET, TACTFNET, PEGDT, PEGNT, FINGAGDT, FINGAGNT.

<u>E</u> LATDOMRM - which included the following variables with the highest loadings: LATDOMHR, LATDOMER, LATDOMFR, LATDOMAR and LATDOMNR.

The results of the factor analyses were most encouraging in that the variables which loaded under each factor in all of the analyses tended to group in meaningful and readily interpretable clusters.

<u>Discriminant Function Analysis</u>

Using the eight criterion groups as an independent variable, the factor scores were subjected to a discriminant function analysis employing SPSS SUB-PROGRAM DISCRIMINANT (Nie <u>et al</u>, 1975) in an attempt to see if there were reliable differences between the groups. That is, this was an attempt to find test patterns which are characteristic of the French immersion group and which differentiate subjects in this group from all seven comparison groups. If a subject could not be correctly assigned to his group, for example, a hyperactive child correctly identified as a hyperactive child and not as a reading disability, this would either indicate that the tests are not sufficiently sensitive to differentiate the subjects or alternatively that there are no test scores or pattern of test scores that can reliably characterize the groups. A failure to reliably classify subjects in this study would not be surprising for a number of reasons. First of all, in the behavioural sciences, research is still at a very early stage and well defined syndromes such as the Turner Syndrome are quite rare. Further, the fact that the eight groups were used rather than a more simple two group discrimination, puts a very heavy burden on the discrimination power of the test battery employed here.

The discriminant function analysis of the eight groups yielded seven discriminant functions to classify the 256 subjects. The eigenvalue, percentage of variance accounted for and significance of each of these discriminant functions are presented in Table V. The first discriminant function accounted for 46.8% of

---

Insert Table V About Here

---

the variance and was significant ($p < .01$). This overall level of significance indicates that there are significant differences among the comparison groups.

It was quite remarkable that a statistically significant number of subjects were correctly classified in each of the eight groups. Table VI presents

---

Insert Table VI About Here

---

the percentage of cases correctly classified in the discriminant analysis of the eight groups. It can be seen that the francophones in francophone schools were

TABLE V

Eigenvalue, Percentage of Variance Accounted for and Significance of the Discriminant Functions in the Eight Group Discriminant Function Analysis

Discriminant Function	Eigenvalue	Relative Percentage	Significance
1	0.4538	46.81	0.00
2	0.18184	21.0	0.00
3	0.11923	13.77	0.006
4	0.09054	10.45	0.097
5	0.03605	4.16	0.540
6	0.02138	2.47	0.624
7	0.01162	1.34	0.585

TABLE VI

Percent of Cases Correctly Classified in the Discriminant Function Analysis of the Eight Groups

Group	Percent Correctly Classified
French immersion	34.4
Anglophones in francophone schools	18.8
Ethnic groups in anglophone schools	31.3
Francophones in francophone schools	62.5
Reading disability	43.8
Hyperactive	18.8
Behaviour and personality problems	28.1
Minimal brain dysfunction	46.9

the easiest to classify (62.5% correctly identified), followed by minimal brain dysfunction (46.9%), reading disability (43.8%), and, fourth, French immersion group (34.4%). The hyperactive and anglophone in francophone school subjects were the most difficult to classify that is, they were spread more widely amongst the other groups. When French immersion children were misclassified, they were misclassified mainly as a reading disability (18.8%), minimal brain dysfunction (18.8%), and hyperactive (12.5%). Analysis of the group membership of subjects who were classified as French immersion included predominantly hyperactive children (18.8%), ethnic groups in anglophone schools (15.6%), and minimal brain dysfunction (12.5%).

The fact that French immersion subjects were significantly differentiated from stringently defined control groups who also experienced difficulty in school gives strong support to the hypothesis that this is a unique group in terms of test profile. This provides strong support for the notion that unique factors are operating in their learning difficulty and that they cannot be considered, as a group, as having origins to their learning problem such as dyslexia, hyperactivity, minimal brain dysfunction or behaviour and personality adjustment problems.

One-Way Analyses of Variance (ANOVA)

In an attempt to identify the factors which differentiated the various groups, further comparisons were made. Since the first discriminant function was significant, there are differences among the groups. The discriminant function analysis also yields F-ratios indicating significance at the level of factors. F-ratios for the ten factors involved in the seven discriminant functions are presented in Table VII. A significant F-ratio indicates that there is a

---

Insert Table VII About Here

---

significant difference between at least two groups on at least one test comprising this factor. To determine these differences the tests loading most highly on the significant factors (Appendix 4) were subjected to one-way analyses of variance employing SPSS SUB-PROGRAM ONE WAY (Nie et al, 1975) with the eight criterion groups as an independent variable. When the overall F-ratio in the ANOVA indicated a significant difference among the eight groups on a particular test, Newman-Keul's test was used to make pairwise comparisons of the group means (Kirk, 1968). The means for each group and the results of the one-way ANOVAS and Newman-Keul's multiple comparisons of the French immersion group with each of the seven comparison groups are presented in Appendix 5.

In order to assure that age and IQ differences were not contributing to the significant between-group differences, an analysis based on restricted age (between 6 and 9) and restricted IQ (WISC Full Scale IQ of between 85 and 109) was made. The means for each of these groups and the results of the one-way ANOVAS and Newman-Keul's multiple comparisons are presented in Appendix 6. The number of subjects in the restricted age and IQ groups are as follows:

French immersion	16
Anglophones in francophone schools	11
Ethnic groups in anglophone schools	11
Francophones in francophone schools	12

TABLE VII

F-ratios for the Factors Comprising the Discriminant Functions in the Discriminant Function Analysis of Eight Groups

Factor	F-ratio[1]
PRFINTOT	3.0375**
ACADTOT	4.7521**
VRBINTOT	4.3077**
PERCTOTA	3.7276**
PERCTOTB	0.9112
TAPMOT	1.4466
PGTACTPT	5.3038**
LATDOMRM	2.2801*
STEADCT	2.0746*
LATDOMLM	2.6275*

[1] The degrees of freedom are 7,248 for all analyses.

*p<.05
**p<.01

Reading disability	15
Hyperactive	20
Behaviour and personality problems	21
Minimal brain dysfunction	16

In this sub-sample there were no significant differences in age or in Full Scale IQ.

As can be seen from Appendix 5, when compared to all subjects in the seven comparison groups the French immersion children generally performed well on the various tests. It must be emphasized that the French immersion group is composed of young, bright children and these children are being compared to seven problem groups, all of whom have had considerable difficulty in school. However, the French immersion children selected for study have had difficulty in school and if one wishes to know whether the basis of this difficulty is related to language factors, then the performance of this group relative to the language comparison groups including group 2 (Anglophones in francophone schools), group 3 (ethnic groups in anglophone schools) and group 4 (francophones in francophone schools) is relevant. However, these children may experience difficulty in French immersion as a result of difficulties independent of the language of instruction. Therefore, comparison with four traditional, classical learning and behavioural difficulty groups such as group 5 (primary reading disability), group 6 (hyperactivity), group 7 (behaviour and personality problems) and group 8 (minimal brain dysfunction) is relevant to this question.

Results of the one-way ANOVAS for the various intelligence, academic achievement, perceptual, motor and sensory tests for the full sample and

restricted age and IQ sub-sample are presented next. A summary of the
significant differences betwen the French immersion group and each of the
seven comparison groups for both the full sample and the restricted age and IQ
sub-sample is presented in Table VIII.

Insert Table VIII About Here
---

1) <u>Intelligence Tests</u>

Group means for various tests of general intelligence are presented
graphically in Figure 1. When all subjects were compared, the French immersion

---
Insert Figure 1 About Here
---

group had a higher performance IQ than the three other language groups (anglophones
in francophone schools, ethnic groups in anglophone schools and francophones in
francophone schools) as well as the hyperactive and minimal brain dysfunction
groups. In addition, the French immersion, reading disability, hyperactive and
behaviour and personality problem groups had significantly higher WISC Verbal IQ
than the three comparison language groups and the French immersion children also
had a significantly higher verbal IQ than the minimal brain dysfunction group.
Thus, the comparison language groups have lower verbal intelligence than three
of the problem groups and the French immersion group. Therefore, low
intelligence may be an important causal factor in the poor performance of the
language groups but not in the French immersion group.

TABLE VIII

Summary of the Significant Differences Between the French Immersion Difficulty Group and Each of the Seven Comparison Groups Based on Newman-Keul's Test

Variables	Full Sample		Restricted Age and IQ	
	Groups Scoring Below the French Immersion Group	Groups Scoring Above the French Immersion Group	Groups Scoring Below the French Immersion Group	Groups Scoring Above the French Immersion Group
PRFINTOT				
WISCPIQ	2,[1.]3,4,6,8			
DEVDRAWT	2,3,4,6,7,8			
ACADTOT				
WRARSS	2,3,4,5,7		2,4	
WRASSS	2,4,5,6,7,8			
VRBINTOT				
WISCVIQ	2,3,4,8			
PEABIQ	2,3,4,8		2,3,4,6,7,8	5
PERCTOTA				
MCANSCAL	4			
BOSTONT	2,3,4		2,4,7	
PGTACTPT				
TPTOTT		3,4,5,6,7		3,4,5,6,7
PEGDT	8		8	
PEGNT	8		8	
TACTFNT	8			
TACTFNET	8			
FINGAGDT	8	7	5,8	
STEADCT				
STEADDCT	3,4			

1. Numbers refer to the groups: 1 (French immersion); 2 (anglophones in francophone schools); 3 (ethnic groups in anglophone schools); 4 (francophones in francophone schools); 5 (reading disability); 6 (hyperactive); 7 (behaviour and personality problems); 8 (minimal brain dysfunction).

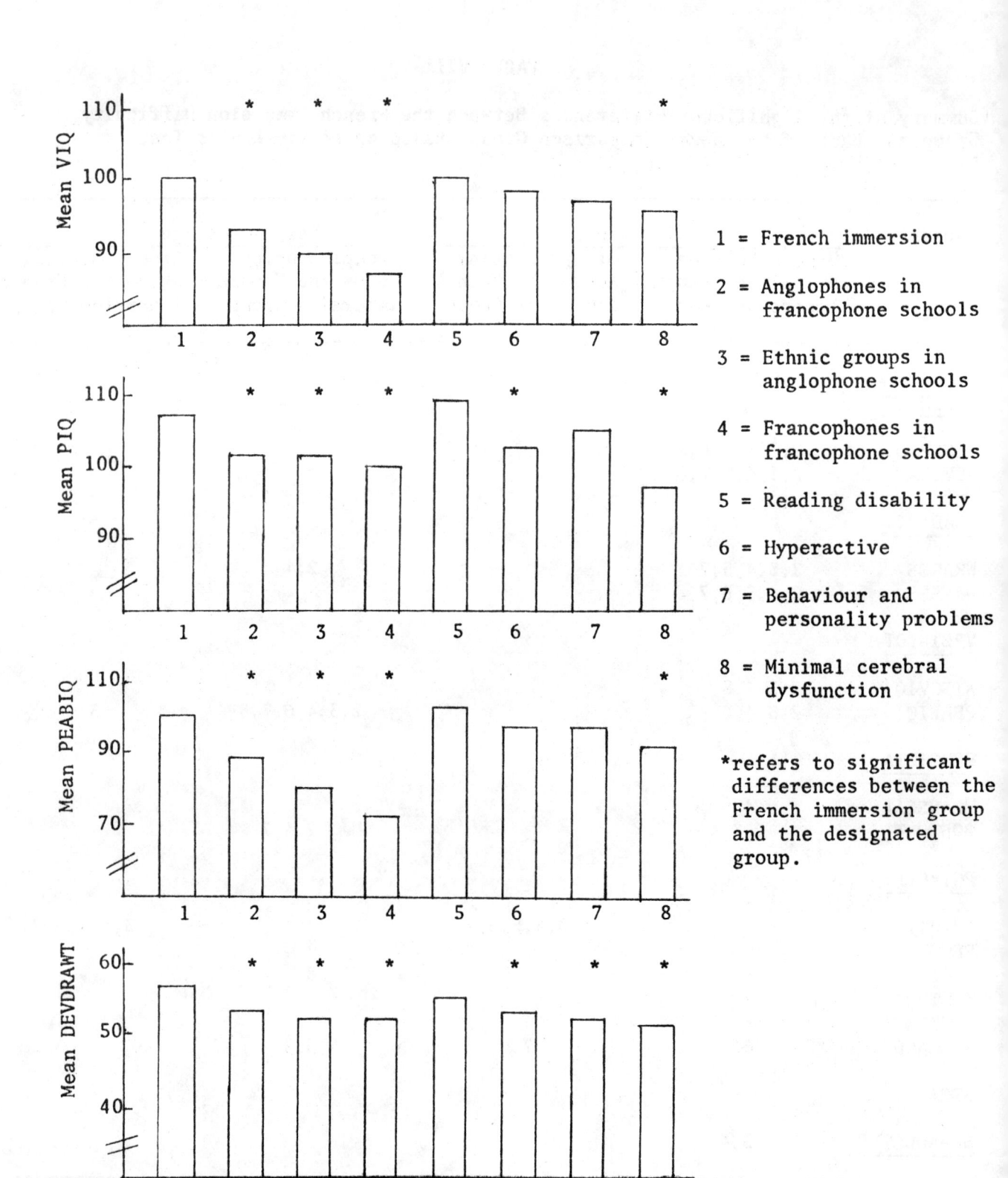

Figure 1: Mean scores obtained by the eight comparison groups on various intelligence tests.

1 = French immersion

2 = Anglophones in francophone schools

3 = Ethnic groups in anglophone schools

4 = Francophones in francophone schools

5 = Reading disability

6 = Hyperactive

7 = Behaviour and personality problems

8 = Minimal cerebral dysfunction

*refers to significant differences between the French immersion group and the designated group.

The French immersion group also had significantly higher scores than all other groups, with the exception of the reading disability group, on the Developmental Drawings copying test. In addition, three of the traditional problem groups and the French immersion group had significantly higher IQ scores on the Peabody Picture Vocabulary Test (a receptive language test) than the three comparison language groups, which again clustered together, and the minimal brain dysfunction group.

However, when age and IQ were restricted (Figure 2) there were no

---

Insert Figure 2 About Here

---

significant differences among the groups in Verbal IQ, Performance IQ or on the Developmental Drawing Test. However, differences were found in vocabulary as measured in the Peabody Picture Vocabulary Test. The reading disability group was significantly superior to all the other groups. The French immersion group, while scoring significantly lower than the reading disability group, had significantly higher performance on the Peabody Picture Vocabulary Test than the remaining six groups.

On the basis of IQ tests alone, the problem seems to be quite different in the French immersion group as compared to the three language control groups. Low IQ is likely implicated in the learning difficulty of the three other language groups but the French immersion group stands out for its high IQ.

2) <u>Academic Achievement Tests</u>

When all subjects were compared on the Wide Range Achievement Tests (WRAT),

1 = French immersion

2 = Anglophones in francophone schools

3 = Ethnic groups in anglophone schools

4 = Francophones in francophone schools

5 = Reading disability

6 = Hyperactive

7 = Behaviour and personality problems

8 = Minimal cerebral dysfunction

*refers to significant differences between the French immersion group and the designated group.

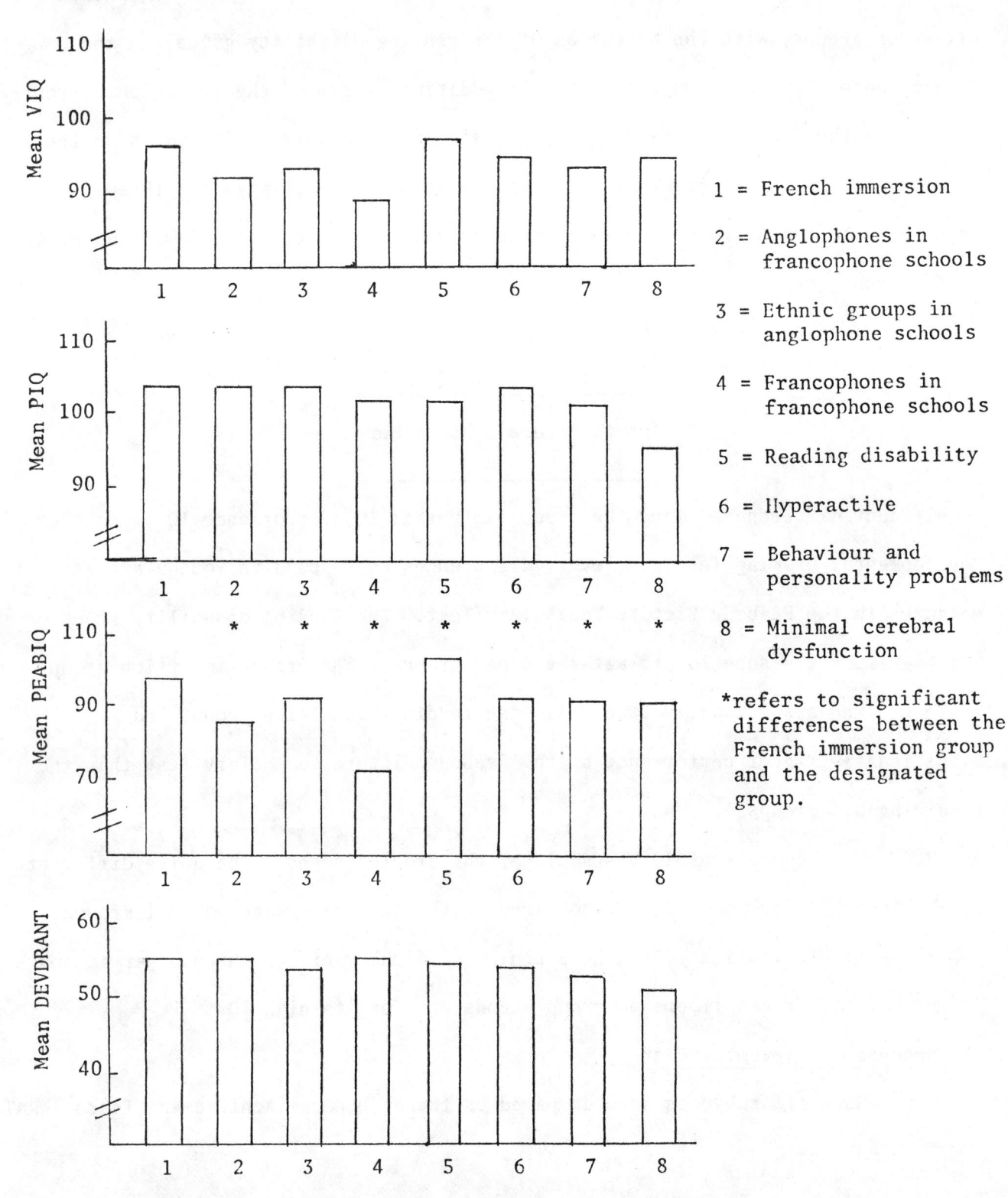

Figure 2: Mean scores obtained by the restricted age and IQ sub-sample on various intelligence tests.

the French immersion group appeard to be performing well academically (Figure 3). Their scores were better than the three language comparison groups, the reading disability group and the behaviour and personality problem group on the WRAT reading test. This comparison was made using scaled scores which are derived for each age level

---

Insert Figure 3 About Here

---

so that a scaled score of 100 corresponds to a score at the 50th percentile for that age group. It is very important to note that although the French immersion group performed best of the eight groups on this measure, their mean scaled score of 94.3 is at the 34th percentile indicating a poor relative academic performance for age. When age and IQ were restricted (Figure 4), the French immersion group

---

Insert Figure 4 About Here

---

performed more poorly (mean scaled score of 88.8 which is at the 21st percentile) and was significantly superior to only anglophones in francophone schools and francophones in francophone schools. It should be stressed that these subjects stay below the 50th percentile as they get older and more will be said of this later. Thus, while French immersion children were found to read better than anglophones in francophone schools, they performed at similar levels to English-speaking children in English schools who have reading disability.

When all children were compared on the WRAT spelling test, the French immersion children significantly outperformed all groups with the exception of ethnic groups in anglophone schools. However, again their mean performance was

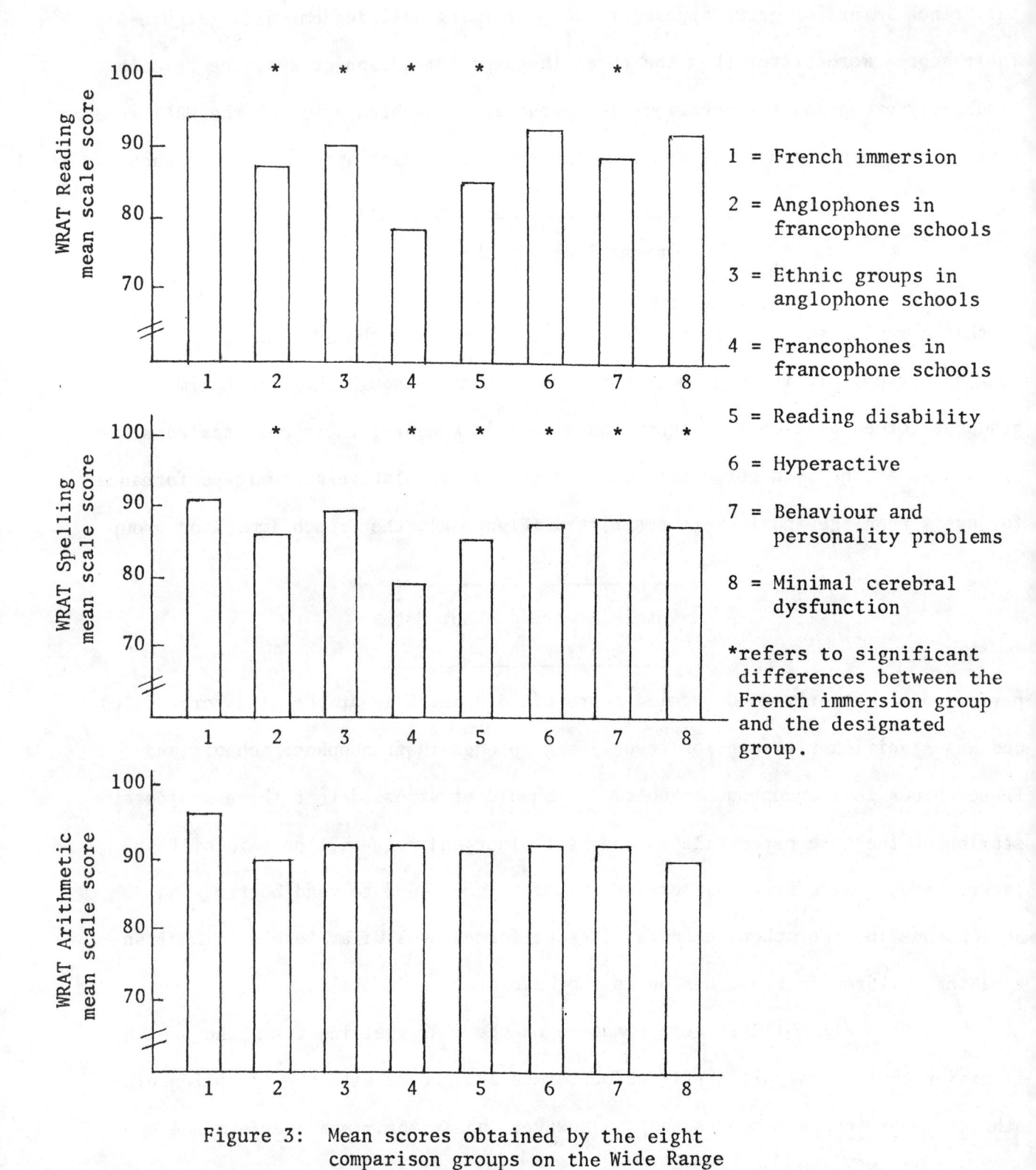

Figure 3: Mean scores obtained by the eight comparison groups on the Wide Range Achievement Tests.

1 = French immersion
2 = Anglophones in francophone schools
3 = Ethnic groups in anglophone schools
4 = Francophones in francophone schools
5 = Reading disability
6 = Hyperactive
7 = Behaviour and personality problems
8 = Minimal cerebral dysfunction

*refers to significant differences between the French immersion group and the designated group.

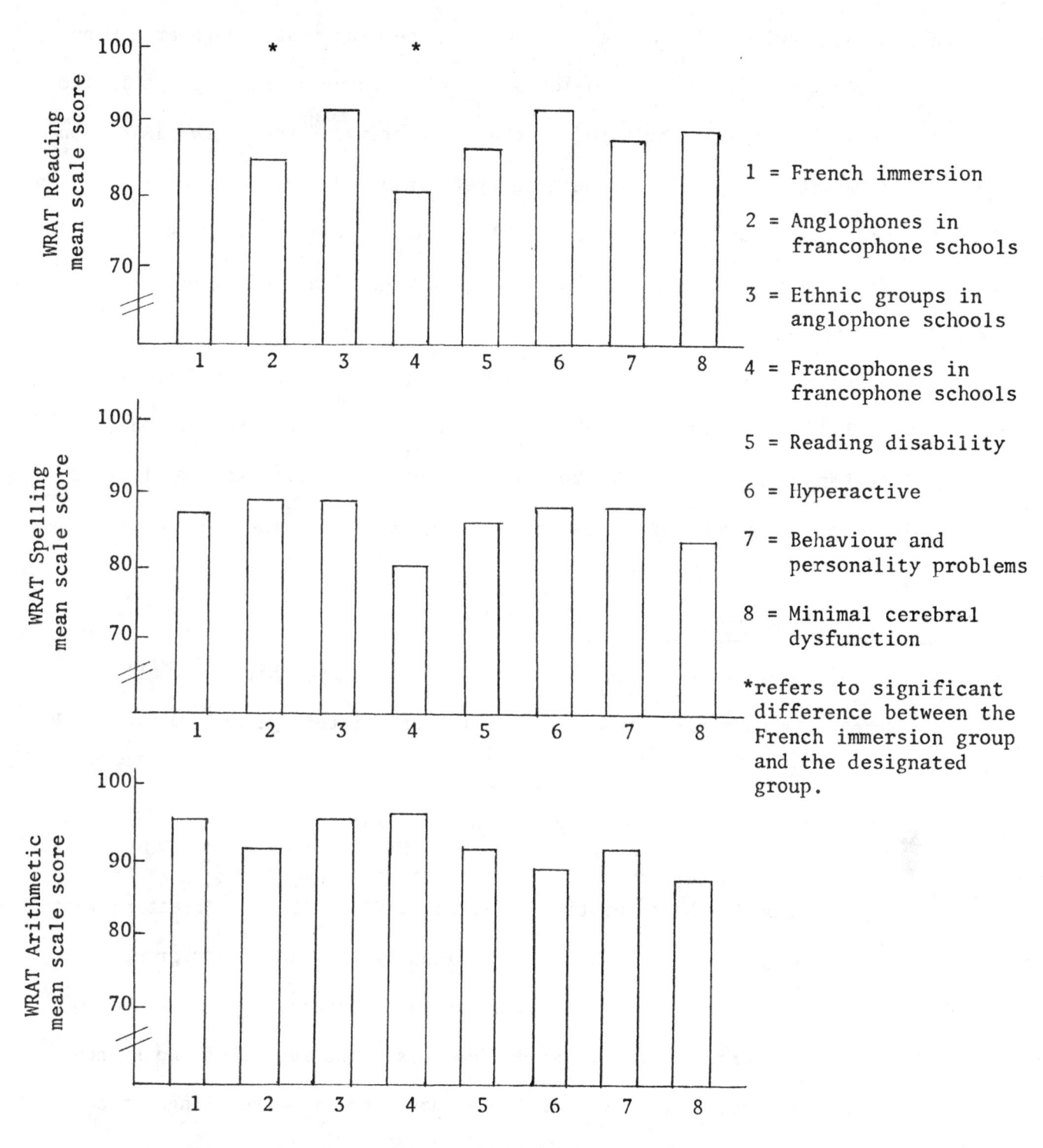

Figure 4: Mean scores obtained by the restricted age and IQ sub-sample on the Wide Range Achievement Tests.

1 = French immersion
2 = Anglophones in francophone schools
3 = Ethnic groups in anglophone schools
4 = Francophones in francophone schools
5 = Reading disability
6 = Hyperactive
7 = Behaviour and personality problems
8 = Minimal cerebral dysfunction

*refers to significant difference between the French immersion group and the designated group.

below the 50th percentile. All differences on the spelling test disappeared when age and IQ were restricted. The inclusion of subjects under 6 years of age in the overall comparison may have contributed to the superiority of the French immersion children since at the early levels, spelling tests involved copying symbols only, and the French immersion group performed very well on this task as well as on the Developmental Drawings Copying Test. There were no significant differences in performance on the arithmetic test.

The French immersion group performed relatively well compared to the learning disability groups on tests of reading and spelling. However, at all times their performance when compared to a normal reference group was far below average which seems even more notable when it is recalled that their IQ's are above average.

3) Auditory Perceptual Abilities

Figure 5 presents the mean scale scores (MCANSCAL) achieved by all subjects in the eight comparison groups and by the restricted age and IQ sub-samples

---

Insert Figure 5 About Here

---

on the Illinois Test of Psycholinguistic Abilities (ITPA). It is interesting that the French immersion group did not differ significantly from any other group, excluding francophones in francophone schools, on this measure. When age and IQ were restricted there were no significant differences. The fact that the French immersion children who have a high Verbal IQ did not excel in psycholinguistic

1 = French immersion

2 = Anglophones in francophone schools

3 = Ethnic groups in anglophone schools

4 = Francophones in francophone schools

5 = Reading disability

6 = Hyperactive

7 = Behaviour and personality problems

8 = Minimal cerebral dysfunction

*refers to significant differences between the French immersion group and the designated group.

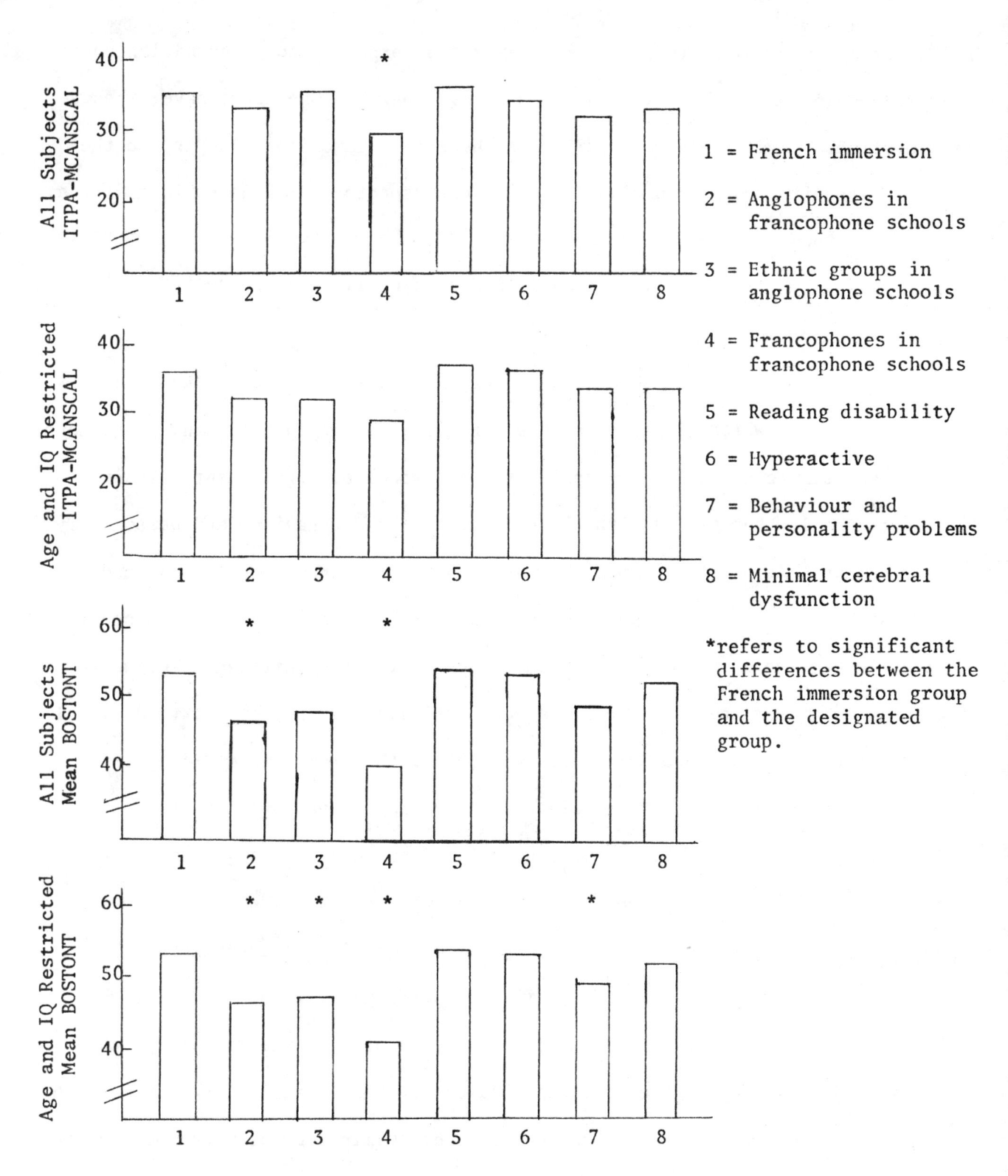

Figure 5: Mean scores obtained by all subjects in the eight comparison groups and by the age and IQ restricted subgroup on tests of auditory perceptual abilities.

abilities as measured by this test indicates that exposure to a second language does not enhance such abilities in one's native tongue. One might have expected well developed psycholinguistic skills in the French immersion group since they are being required to attend closely to various aspects of language. In addition, poor psycholinguistic abilities did not appear to be related to poor progress in a second language and we will monitor Illinois psycholinguistic scores carefully in our further follow-up.

On a measure of speech-sound discrimination ability (Boston Speech Perception Test), which is also presented in Figure 5, anglophones in francophone schools and ethnic groups in anglophone schools received significantly lower scores than all other groups with the exception of the behaviour and personality problem group. As might be expected, francophones in francophone schools had the lowest scores but they were penalized as a result of language factors, since this test is in English only. The French immersion children significantly outperformed the language groups and performed in a manner similar to that of the traditional problem groups. When age and IQ were restricted, the French immersion group continued to perform at levels similar to three traditional problem groups (excluding the behaviour and personality problem group) and outperformed anglophones in francophone schools and francophones in francophone schools. However, it is important to note that all eight groups performed fairly poorly on this test. Although little normative data are available, performance levels of the eight groups are probably in the lower quartile. The results of the Boston Speech Perception Test could be interpreted as indicating that familiarity with more than one language does not facilitate speech sound discrimination as might be expected following exposure to many more speech sounds and the need to discriminate amongst them. However, this will be looked at carefully in a further follow-up of good and poor performers in a second language program.

4) Motor and Sensory Tests

It can be seen from Figure 6 that the French immersion group significantly

---

Insert Figure 6 About Here

---

outperformed ethnic groups in anglophone schools and francophones in francophone schools on a measure of resting tremor (STEADDCT). In addition, the French immersion group outperformed the minimal brain dysfunction group on measures of fine-manipulative skills (PEGDT, PEGNT). As can be seen from Figure 7, the French

---

Insert Figure 7 About Here

---

immersion group performed at significantly higher levels than the minimal brain dysfunction group on other sensory and sensory motor measures (TACTFNET, TACTFNT, FINGAGDT) and at a significantly lower level than the behavour and personality problem group on a fingertip recognition measure (FINGAGDT). When age and IQ were restricted, the French immersion group continued to outperform the minimal brain dysfunction group on measures of fingertip recognition and fine manipulative skills. Only the minimal brain dysfunction group showed consistent deficits on sensory and sensory motor measures while the French immersion group performed within essentially normal limits.

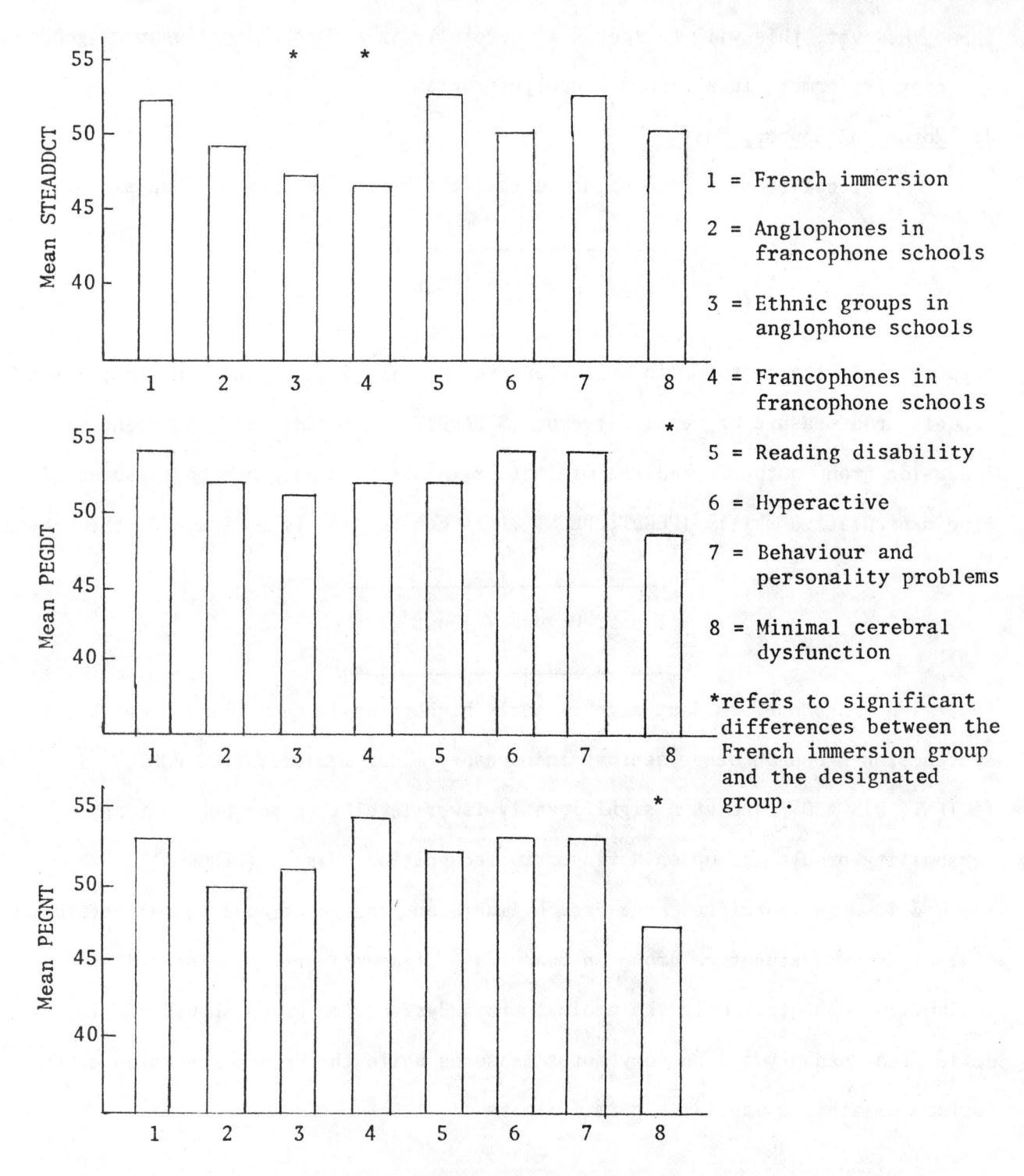

Figure 6: Mean scores obtained by the eight comparison groups on certain motor tests.

1 = French immersion
2 = Anglophones in francophone schools
3 = Ethnic groups in anglophone schools
4 = Francophones in francophone schools
5 = Reading disability
6 = Hyperactive
7 = Behaviour and personality problems
8 = Minimal cerebral dysfunction

*refers to significant differences between the French immersion group and the designated group.

1 = French immersion

2 = Anglophones in francophone schools

3 = Ethnic groups in anglophone schools

4 = Francophones in francophone schools

5 = Reading disability

6 = Hyperactive

7 = Behaviour and personality problems

8 = Minimal cerebral dysfunction

*refers to significant differences between the French immersion group and the designated group.

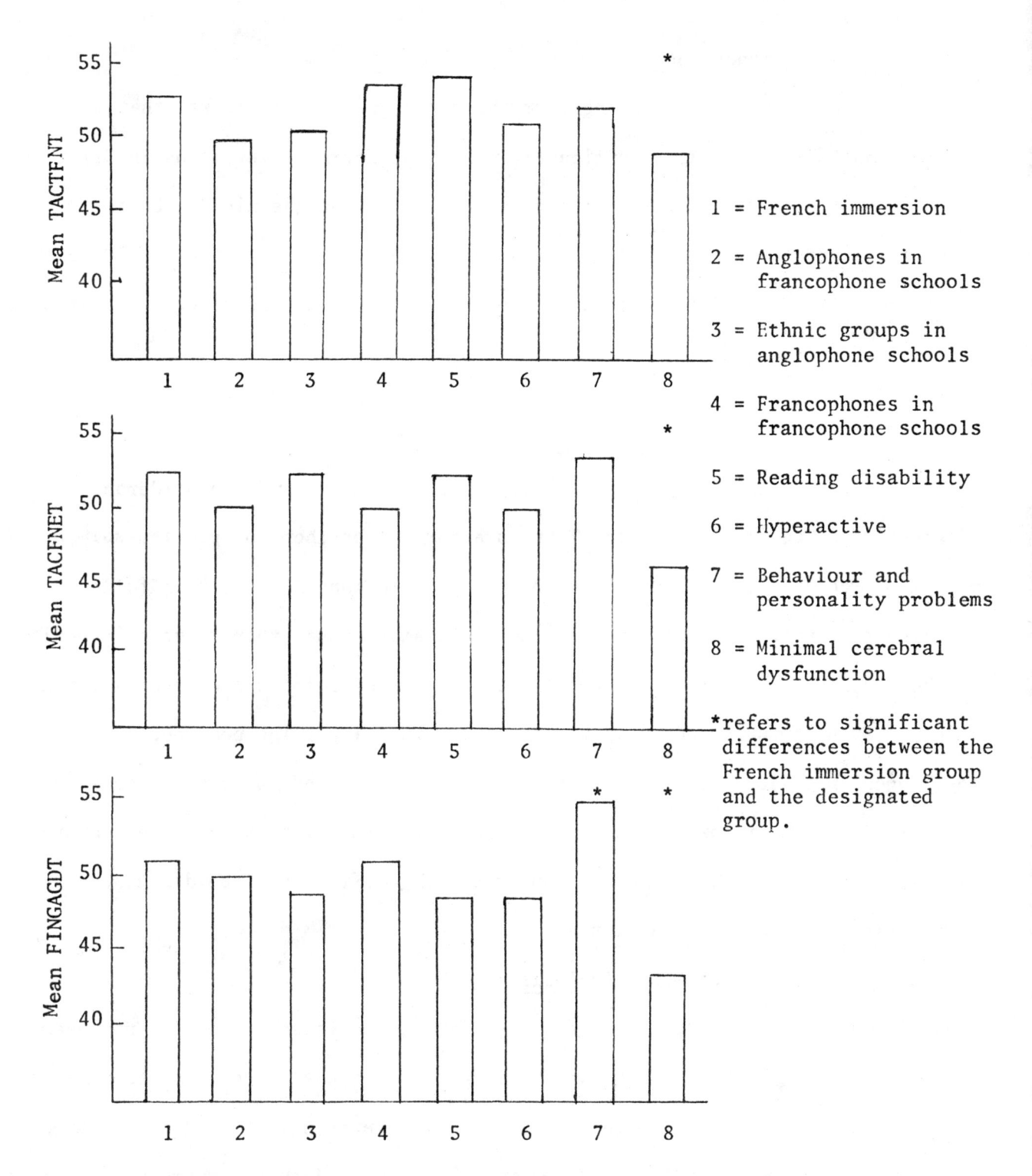

Figure 7: Mean scaled scores obtained on certain sensory and motor tests.

5) Tactual Performance Test

A most important finding from the eight group analysis was that the French immersion group had significantly poorer performance levels on TPTOTT than all groups except anglophones in francophone schools and the minimal brain dysfunction group both when all subjects were compared and when age and IQ were restricted (Figure 8). The fact that the French immersion group performed at poor

---

Insert Figure 8 About Here

---

levels similar to the brain damaged group on this measure is of considerable interest. The Tactual Performance Test is a complex psychomotor problem-solving task in which the subject must place blocks in a formboard while blindfolded. Adequate performance on this task is dependent among other things, upon integrity of the temporal lobes and it is known that the temporal lobes are important brain structures in language and auditory-perceptual functions. The poor performance of the French immersion group cannot be considered as related to motor or sensory deficits since their performance was well within normal limits on these measures. The importance of the psychomotor problem-solving deficit will be discussed further in the discussion section.

6) Summary of the Eight Group Analysis

Based on the results of the eight group analysis, there does not seem to be a single factor or measure which differentiates the French immersion group from all other groups. Although this is hardly surprising, it should be stated clearly that, although subjects can be reliably assigned to their groups and there

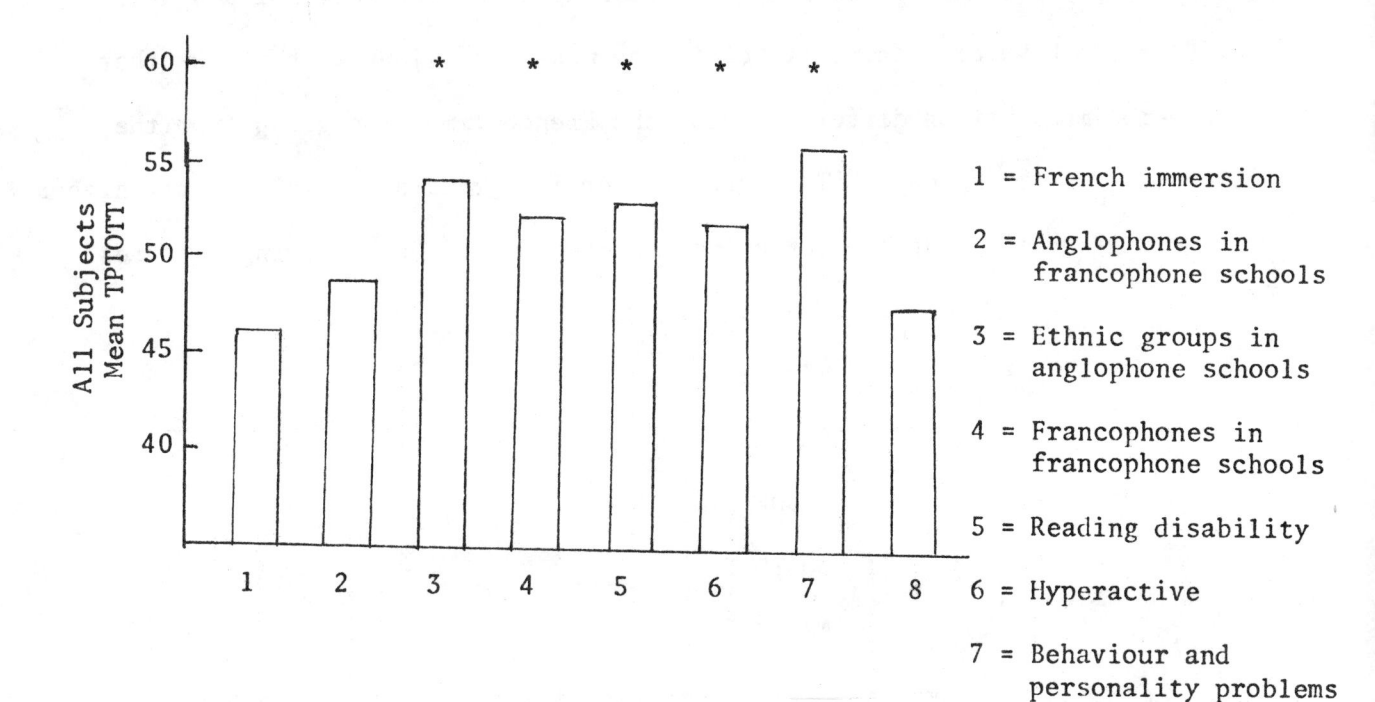

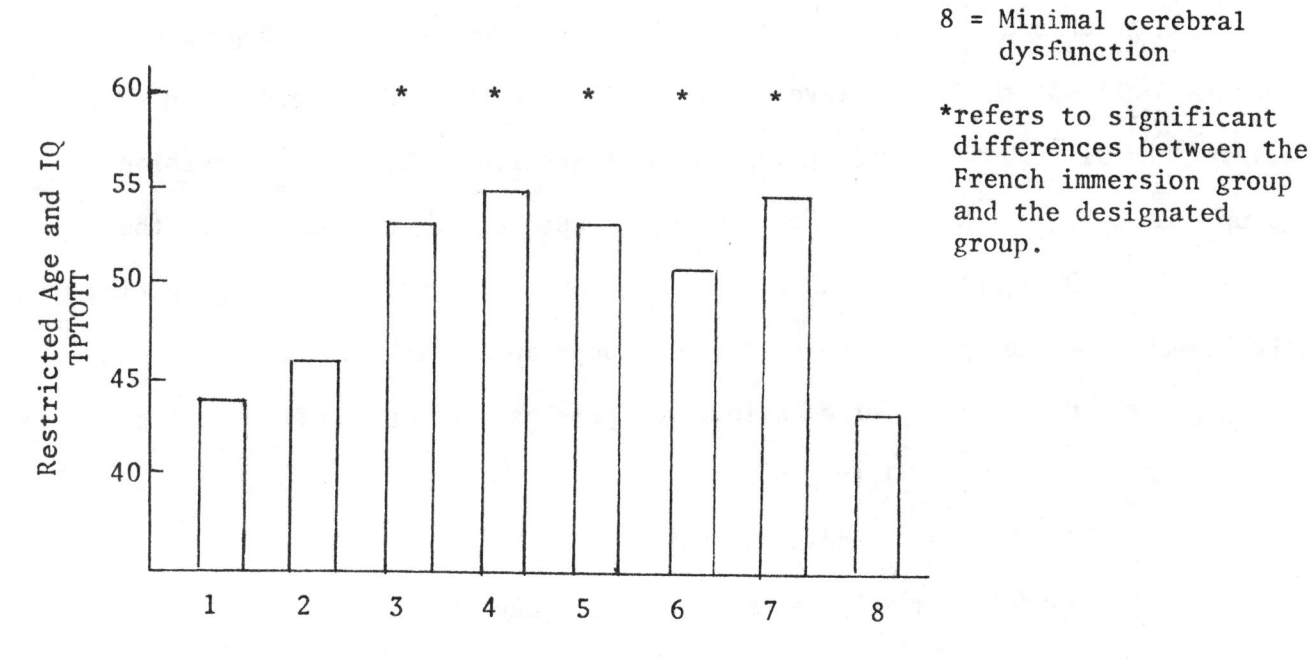

Figure 8: Mean scores on the TPTOTT measure for the eight comparison groups and for the restircted age and IQ sub-sample.

1 = French immersion
2 = Anglophones in francophone schools
3 = Ethnic groups in anglophone schools
4 = Francophones in francophone schools
5 = Reading disability
6 = Hyperactive
7 = Behaviour and personality problems
8 = Minimal cerebral dysfunction

*refers to significant differences between the French immersion group and the designated group.

are clear group differences this cannot be determined on the basis of a single test or factor. However, general intelligence measures, along with a few other measures were important in differentiating the French immersion group from the three language control groups. The French immersion group had significantly higher scores (Newman-Kuels), than the three language groups on the following measures:

        WISCVIQ

        WISCPIQ

        PEABIQ

        DEVDRAWT

        BOSTONT

        WRARSS

Academic tests may also be a good discriminator between the French immersion group and all other groups since the French immersion group outperformed all but the hyperactive and minimal brain dysfunction groups on WRAT reading and all but the ethnic groups on WRAT spelling. The French immersion group scored higher than all other groups, except reading disability, on the Developmental Drawings Test. Thus, the most important tests for discrminating the French immersion group from all other groups appear to be:

    WISCPIQ (except for behaviour and personality problem and reading
        disability groups)

    DEVDRAWT (except reading disability)

    WRAT spelling (except ethnic groups in anglophone schools)

    WRAT reading (except hyperactive and minimal brain dysfunction
        groups)

PEABIQ (except reading disability, hyperactive and behaviour
and personality problem groups)

Two-Group Discriminant Function Analyses

Following the eight group discriminant function analysis, seven independent two-group discriminant function analyses were performed comparing the French immersion group with each of the other seven comparison groups. For each analysis, group means for measures which had the highest loadings on the significant factors were compared by means of t-tests. In general, it can be stated that the French immersion group is highly significantly different from all other seven groups. In these comparisons, 71.9% to 84.4% of the French immersion subjects were correctly classified. Table IX summarizes the percent of cases correctly classified in each of the two-group discriminant function

---

Insert Table IX About Here

---

analyses. The mean probability that a certain subject will be correctly classified in the group to which he belongs is also presented in Table IX.

In all comparisons the French immersion group had the highest scores except for one difference in the French immersion versus ethnic groups in anglophone schools (LATDOMHR) and French immersion versus the behaviour and personality problem group (FINGER AGNOSIA) comparisons. The following seven tables, one for each two-group comparison, list the significant factors in the discriminant function and under each factor the significant tests, their means, standard deviations and t-probability.

TABLE IX

Percent of Cases Correctly Classified in the Discriminant Function
Analyses Involving Two Groups

Groups Compared	Percent Correctly Classified	Probability
French immersion vs.	71.9	0.6047
Anglophones in francophone schools	68.8	0.6028
TOTAL	70.3	
French immersion vs.	71.9	0.6626
Ethnic groups in anglophone schools	81.3	0.6806
TOTAL	76.6	
French immersion vs.	78.1	0.7528
Francophones in francophone schools	90.6	0.7925
TOTAL	84.4	
French immersion vs.	71.9	0.6132
Reading disability	75.0	0.6312
TOTAL	73.4	
French immersion vs.	75.0	0.6271
Hyperactive	71.9	0.6276
TOTAL	73.4	
French immersion vs.	84.4	0.6823
Behaviour and personality problems	81.3	0.6802
TOTAL	82.8	
French immersion vs.	75.0	0.6309
Minimal brain damage	71.9	0.6113
TOTAL	73.4	

In Table X, it can be seen that in the differentiation between the

---
Insert Table X About Here

French immersion group and anglophones in francophone schools, auditory perceptual measures were very important, particularly the ITPA and Boston Speech Perception Test along with academic achievement scores for reading and arithmetic and certain performance IQ measures such as Raven Progressive Matrices and Developmental Drawings.

Table XI presents differences between groups based on the discriminant function analysis between the French immersion group and the ethnic groups in

---
Insert Table XI About Here
---

anglophone schools. It can be seen that the most important differentiating variables here were verbal intelligence factors (WISCVIQ, PEABIQ) along with the Developmental Drawings Test and various motor measures.

Table XII presents the comparison between the French immersion group and the francophones in francophone schools. The academic measures (WRAT reading

---
Insert Table XII About Here
---

and spelling) along with both verbal and non-verbal intelligence measures were the most discriminating tests.

TABLE X

Discriminant Function Analysis:[1] French Immersion Group (1) vs.
Anglophones in Francophone Schools (2)

Factors	Significant Tests	$Mean_1$	$S.D._1$	$Mean_2$	$S.D._2$	t-Prob.
1) PERCTOTA	ITPA (MCANSCAL)	36.0	3.7	32.3	6.8	0.007
	BOSTON SPEECH PERCEPTION TEST	53.0	8.7	46.3	9.6	0.015
2) ACADTOT						
	Wide Range Achievement Test:					
	Reading	94.3	10.6	87.4	11.7	0.016
	Arithmetic	97.6	10.1	90.8	9.6	0.007
3) PRFINTOT						
	MATRICES	54.8	7.9	49.2	7.8	0.011
	DEVELOPMENTAL DRAWINGS	57.4	7.0	53.5	7.6	0.039
4) LATDOMRM						

[1] Discriminant function: probability=0.007

TABLE XI

Discriminant Function Analysis:[1.] French Immersion Group (1) vs. Ethnic Groups in Anglophone Schools (3)

Factors	Significant Tests	Mean$_1$	S.D.$_1$	Mean$_3$	S.D.$_3$	t-Prob.
1) VRBINTOT						
	WISC VERBAL IQ	100.9	11.6	89.9	12.3	0.000
	PEABODY IQ	100.3	16.4	80.1	17.0	0.007
2) LATDOMRM						
	LATDOMHR	5.2	2.7	6.7	1.0	0.004
	LATDOMNR	19.9	14.3	13.7	7.5	0.038
3) MAZECT						
	MAZENCT	56.9	9.1	51.7	7.9	0.022
	MAZEDCT	58.1	7.0	52.6	7.2	0.004
4) PRFINTOT						
	DEVELOPMENTAL DRAWINGS	57.4	7.0	52.2	8.5	0.010
5) PGTACTPT						
	PEGDT	54.7	5.9	51.5	6.7	0.047

[1.] Discriminant function: probability=0.000

TABLE XII

Discriminant Function Analysis:[1] French Immersion Group (1) vs.
Francophones in Francophone Schools (4)

Factors	Significant Tests	Mean$_1$	S.D.$_1$	Mean$_4$	S.D.$_4$	t-Prob.
1) ACADTOT						
	Wide Range Achievement Test:					
	Reading	94.3	10.6	78.1	7.2	0.000
	Spelling	91.8	11.2	79.0	5.3	0.000
2) PRFINTOT						
	WISC PERFORMANCE IQ	107.5	10.9	100.0	10.8	0.008
	DEVELOPMENTAL DRAWINGS	57.4	7.0	52.1	7.4	0.005
3) PGTACTPT						
4) PERCTOT B						
5) LATDOMLM						
	LATDOMHL	1.8	2.7	0.5	1.4	0.019
6) VRBINTOT						
	WISC VERBAL IQ	100.9	11.6	88.6	12.2	0.000
	PEABODY IQ	100.3	16.3	72.5	9.3	0.000

[1] Discriminant Function: probability=0.000

In comparing the French immersion group with the reading disability group in Table XIII only the academic achievement scores for reading, spelling and

---
Insert Table XIII About Here
---

arithmetic discriminated between the two groups.

In differentiating the French immersion group from the hyperactive group, as can be seen in Table XIV, the differences were accounted for mainly on the basis of non-verbal performance measures including spatial construction ability and

---
Insert Table XIV About Here
---

non-verbal reasoning (Halstead Category Test, Raven Progressive Matrices Test).

Table XV presents the comparison between the French immersion and the behaviour and personality problem group, in which the behaviour problem group

---
Insert Table XV About Here
---

performed at better levels on a fingertip recognition measure (Finger Agnosia) but poorer on tests of motor function (MAZEDCT), academic achievement levels for reading and arithmetic as well as a spatial construction task (Developmental Drawings Test).

Lastly, Table XVI presents the results of the discriminant function analysis between the French immersion and minimal brain dysfunction groups in which

TABLE XIII

Discriminant Function Analysis:[1] French Immersion Group (1) vs. Reading Disability (5)

Factors	Significant Tests	Mean$_1$	S.D.$_1$	Mean$_5$	S.D.$_5$	t-Prob.
1) ACADTOT						
	Wide Range Achievement Test:					
	Reading	94.3	10.6	85.9	7.6	0.001
	Spelling	91.8	11.2	85.6	7.5	0.011
	Arithmetic	97.6	10.1	91.9	8.6	0.018
2) MAZECT						
3) STEADCT						
4) PGTACTPT						

[1] Discriminant function: probability=0.002

TABLE XIV

Discriminant Function Analysis:[1] French Immersion Group (1) vs. Hyperactive (6)

Factors	Significant Tests	Mean$_1$	S.D.$_1$	Mean$_6$	S.D.$_6$	t-Prob.
1) PRFINTOT						
	MATRICES	54.8	7.9	49.7	7.6	0.018
	DEVELOPMENTAL DRAWINGS	57.4	7.0	53.0	8.1	0.026
	HALSTEAD CATEGORY	54.3	8.5	48.7	7.9	0.012
2) PERCTOTA						
3) VERGMOT						
4) LATDOMRM						
5) VRBINTOT						
6) PGTACTPT						

[1] Discriminant function: probability=0.009

TABLE XV

Discriminant Function Analysis:[1.] French Immersion Group (1) vs.
Behaviour and Personality Problems (7)

Factors	Significant Tests	Mean$_1$	S.D.$_1$	Mean$_7$	S.D.$_7$	t-Prob.
1) PGTACTPT						
	FINGER AGNOSIA (Dominant Hand)	51.1	7.4	55.2	5.8	0.018
2) LATDOMRM						
3) STEADCT						
4) MAZECT						
	MAZEDCT	58.1	7.0	54.9	5.4	0.050
5) LATDOMHL						
6) PRFINTOT						
	DEVELOPMENTAL DRAWINGS	57.4	7.0	52.7	7.2	0.011
7) ACADTOT						
	Wide Range Achievement Test:					
	Reading	94.3	10.6	88.8	11.2	0.049
	Arithmetic	97.6	10.1	92.2	7.7	0.019
8) PERCTOTA						

[1.] Discriminant Function: probability=0.002

Insert Table XVI About Here
---

there were many differentiating tests including performance intelligence along with several sensory and motor measures.

In looking for trends in the various two-group discriminant function analyses it is important to note that reading achievement levels were particularly low for the anglophones in francophone schools, francophones in francophone schools, reading disability group and behaviour-personality adjustment problem groups. The factor comprised of performance intelligence measures was important in the differentiation of the French immersion group from all but the reading disability group. In contrast, the WISCVIQ and Peabody IQ tests of the verbal intelligence factor were important in differentiating between the French immersion group and two language groups, namely, ethnic groups in anglophone schools and francophones in francophone schools. This verbal dimension may be an important aspect of the learning problem of these two language groups but not of the French immersion group.

The most important finding, however, is presented in Table IX, namely the very high percentage of correct classifications in each of the two-group comparisons.

Verbal IQ - Performance IQ Differences

It could be observed earlier (Figure 1 and Figure 2) that for all groups there was a tendency for the mean scores for the Wechsler Intelligence Scale for Children (WISC) Performance IQ to be higher than for the WISC Verbal IQ. The

TABLE XVI

Discriminant Function Analysis:[1.] French Immersion Group (1) vs. Minimal Brain Dysfunction (8)

Factors	Significant Tests	Mean$_1$	S.D.$_1$	Mean$_8$	S.D.$_8$	t-Prob.
1) PRFINTOT						
	WISC PERFORMANCE IQ	107.5	10.9	97.8	13.5	0.002
	DEVELOPMENTAL DRAWINGS	57.4	7.0	51.6	8.4	0.004
2) PGTACTPT						
	PEGDT	54.7	5.9	48.4	9.7	0.003
	PEGNT	53.4	5.8	47.2	12.6	0.014
	FINGER AGNOSIA (Dominant)	51.1	7.4	43.2	12.3	0.004
	TACTILE FORMS (Nondominant)	52.5	5.9	48.3	10.1	0.050
3) PERCTOT B						
4) MAZECT						
	MAZENCT	56.9	9.1	48.4	11.5	0.003
	MAZEDCT	58.1	7.0	50.3	9.7	0.001

[1.] Discriminant Function: probability=0.002

difference between the Verbal IQ and Performance IQ was calculated for all groups subtracting VIQ from PIQ and calculating the means of the difference scores. Significant group differences were indicated in a one-way ANOVA (F=2.939, df=8,255, p<.01). Pairwise comparisons between the French immersion group and each of the seven comparison groups as well as a small French immersion success group, were carried out using Newman-Keul's Test. The mean diffference score for each group and the results of the multiple comparisons are presented in Table XVII. It should

---

Insert Table XVII About Here

---

be noted that the largest Verbal-Performance discrepancies are noted for ethnic groups in anglophone schools, and francophones in francophone schools with the reading disability groups also showing a very large difference. There was a lesser tendency for the two other language groups, namely, French immersion children and anglophones in francophone schools to show a Verbal-Performance discrepancy. One could consider that for ethnic groups in anglophone schools and francophones in francophone schools, the difficulty in school progress could be attributed to a language deficit which is seen also, but to a slightly lesser extent, in the reading disability group. It is interesting to note that the French immersion success group, which is a small sample of eight subjects who were progressing well in their French immersion class and will be discussed later for comparison purposes, had the smallest discrepancy and is the only group which can be characterized as not having any subjects who are having difficulty in school.

TABLE XVII

Mean Difference Scores (WISCPIQ - WISCVIQ) for the Eight Comparison Groups
and the French Immersion Success Group

Group	Mean Difference Score
French immersion	6.5938
Anglophones in francophone schools	7.9688
Ethnic groups in anglophone schools	12.3125*[1]
Francophones in francophone schools	11.5313*
Reading Disability	9.0938
Hyperactive	4.8438
Behaviour and personality problems	8.5938
Minimal brain dysfunction	0.9688*
French immersion success	0.2500*

[1] The significant differences indicated refer only to pairwise comparisons involving the French immersion group.

* $p < .05$

FOLLOW-UP OF THE FRENCH IMMERSION SAMPLE

In addition to the complete neuropsychological test profiles on all children in French immersion, both those having difficulty and the small group experiencing success, considerable additional information was systematically obtained. This included extensive history data, personality tests and behaviour rating scales completed by both parents and teachers.

Some subjects were also brought in for retesting on various psychometric and academic achievement tests. This follow-up testing was considered to be a significant part of this study since some of the important questions could only be answered by follow-up assessment. These questions included: Do children who have difficulty in French immersion have continuing difficulty when they are switched to an English program?; What is the outcome for children having difficulty in a French immersion program who are maintained in a French immersion program?; Do children who are initially successful in French immersion continue to progress well in the program?

At the time of retest, questionnaire forms developed specifically for this research project (Appendix 3) were completed along with a family history of reading problems and retest behaviour ratings by parents and teachers (Appendix 2).

Of the 32 subjects in the French immersion difficulty group, 24 were retested. These children were subdivided into three groups, namely, 11 children who had difficulty in French immersion, but were still in the program (French immersion-French immersion group); seven children who were in French immersion at the time of first testing, but had been switched to the English program since first testing (French immersion-English group); and six children who had experienced difficulty in French immersion, but were in an English language program at the time of both testings (English-English group). For comparison purposes, a fourth group was composed of children who were not having difficulty in French immersion (French immersion success group). Seven of the eight children in this group were retested.

Amnestic, Attitudinal, Behavioural and Personality Data

1) Connors Parent's Questionnaire (Appendix 2)

The Connors Rating Scales for parents and teachers are widely used measures which provide ratings of hyperactivity, attentiveness, impulsivity, conduct problem, tension and anxiety as these behavioural characteristics relate to home as well as school behaviour.

    a) Comparison of the Total French Immersion Difficulty Group and the French Immersion Success Group:

The parent ratings of the French immersion difficulty group and the French immersion success group on first testing are presented in Figure 9. The means, standard deviations and t-probabilities for this comparison are presented

---

Insert Figure 9 About Here

---

in Table XVIII. There were no significant differences between the two groups

---

Insert Table XVIII About Here

(t-tests computed on percent scores) on the first testing. There was a non-significant tendency for the French immersion difficulty group to obtain a higher score on the learning problem scale and for the French immersion success group to

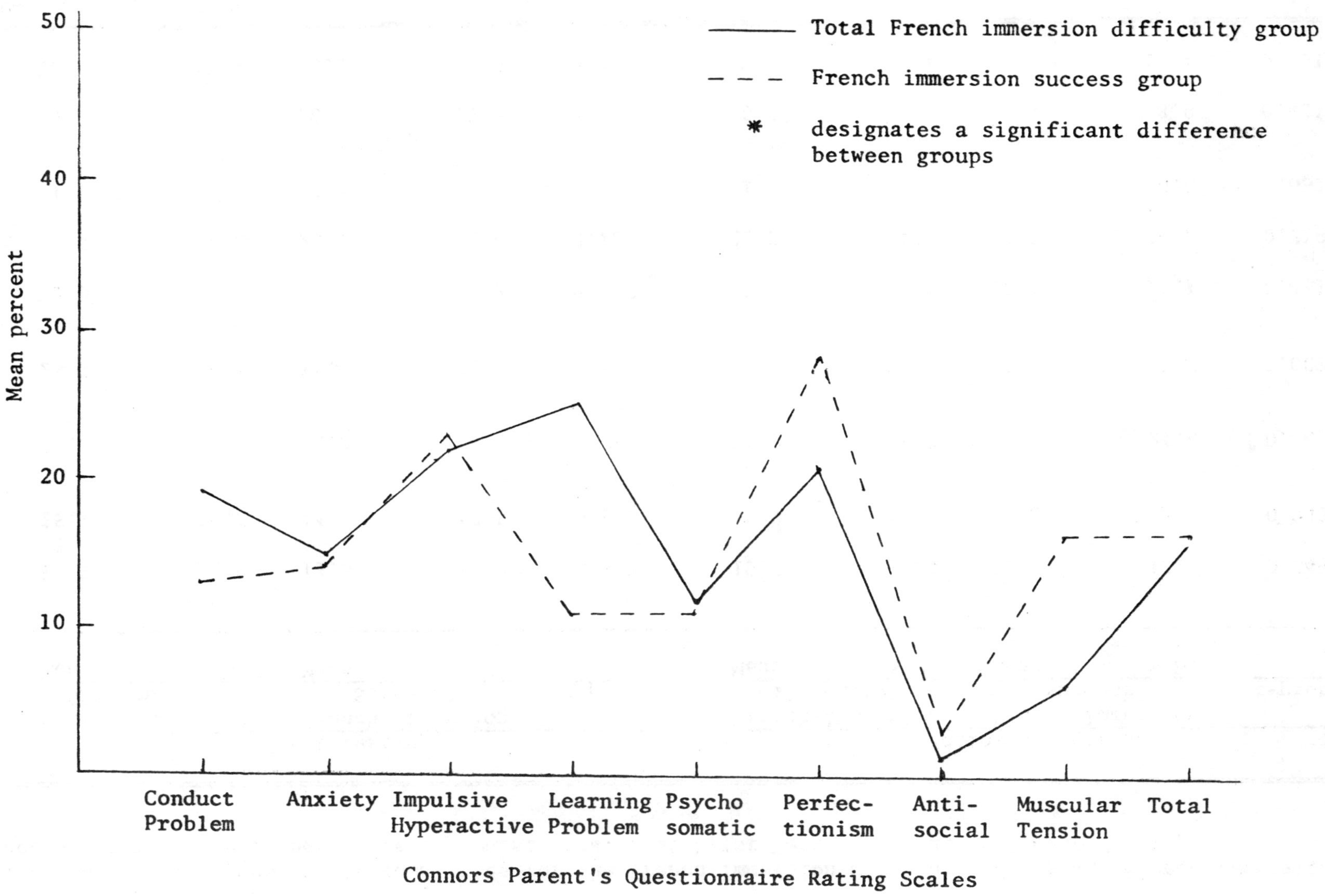

Figure 9: Connors Parent's Symptom Questionnaire ratings of the total French immersion difficulty group and the French immersion success group at first testing.

TABLE XVIII

Mean Ratings, Standard Deviations and t-probabilities for the French Immersion Difficulty Group and French Immersion Success Group on the Connors Parent's Questionnaire at First Testing and at Follow-up Testing

Rating Scales	First Testing							Follow-up Testing				
	French Immersion Difficulty[1]		French Immersion Success[2]		t-prob.	French Immersion Difficulty[3]		French Immersion Success[4]		t-prob.
	Mean	S.D.	Mean	S.D.		Mean	S.D.	Mean	S.D.	
Conduct Problem	19.7	20.9	13.3	11.7	0.413	19.7	13.5	17.0	13.1	0.649
Anxiety	15.1	16.5	14.3	13.5	0.917	15.9	13.5	16.3	16.7	0.942
Impulsive-Hyperactive	22.6	14.4	23.3	34.0	0.943	21.9	18.7	29.7	24.6	0.462
Learning Problem	23.7	15.3	11.7	21.7	0.304	22.3	20.1	5.9	9.3	0.007**
Psychosomatic	12.9	15.9	11.9	8.7	0.873	8.2	10.1	10.5	12.1	0.661
Perfectionism	21.4	31.6	28.9	42.0	0.729	23.2	24.9	19.0	26.2	0.718
Anti-Social	1.8	4.8	3.4	7.1	0.675	1.9	4.4	0.0	0.0	0.057
Muscular Tension	5.9	6.1	16.7	23.6	0.371	6.8	7.1	9.5	8.9	0.481
Total	16.5	11.4	16.8	11.0	0.966	15.7	8.4	17.8	10.4	0.651

[1]. N=12   [2]. N=5   [3]. N=22   [4]. N=7
**p<.01

have a higher score on the perfectionism scale. Both groups obtained fairly high scores on the impulsivity-hyperactivity scale. The means, standard deviations and t-probabilities for these groups at follow-up testing are also presented in Table XVIII.

On second testing, the French immersion difficulty group obtained a significantly higher score on the learning problem scale (Figure 10). No other differences approached significance, although, interestingly, the French immersion

---

Insert Figure 10 About Here

---

success group obtained a higher score on the impulsivity-hyperactivity scale.

    b) Comparison of the three French Immersion Difficulty Sub-groups and the French Immersion Success Group:

Figure 11 presents comparisons of the parent ratings obtained by the

---

Insert Figure 11 About Here

---

three French immersion difficulty sub-groups and the French immersion success group on the Connors Parent's Questionnaire at follow-up testing. The relevant means and standard deviations are presented in Table XIX. The only significant

---

Insert Table XIX About Here

---

difference was a very high score on the learning problem scale for those French immersion difficulty children who were in French immersion at the time of first testing and had been switched to an English language program by the follow-up

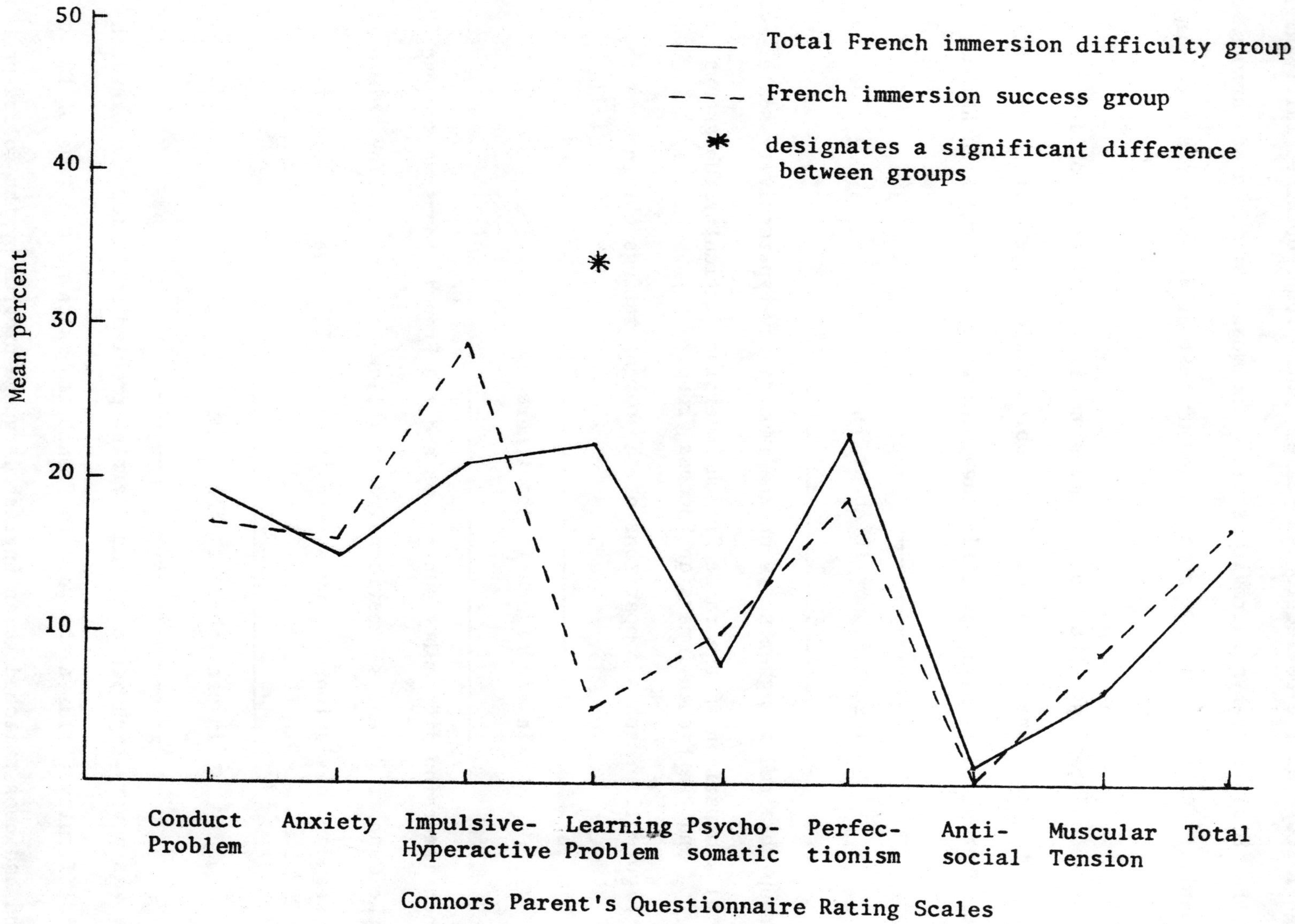

82

Conduct   Anxiety Impulsive- Learning Psycho-   Perfec-   Anti-   Muscular Total
Problem   Hyperactive Problem   somatic   tionism   social   Tension

—— Total French immersion difficulty group
--- French immersion success group
* designates a significant difference between groups

Connors Parent's Questionnaire Rating Scales

Figure 10: Connors Parent's Symptom Questionnaire ratings of the total French immersion difficulty group and the French immersion success group at follow-up testing.

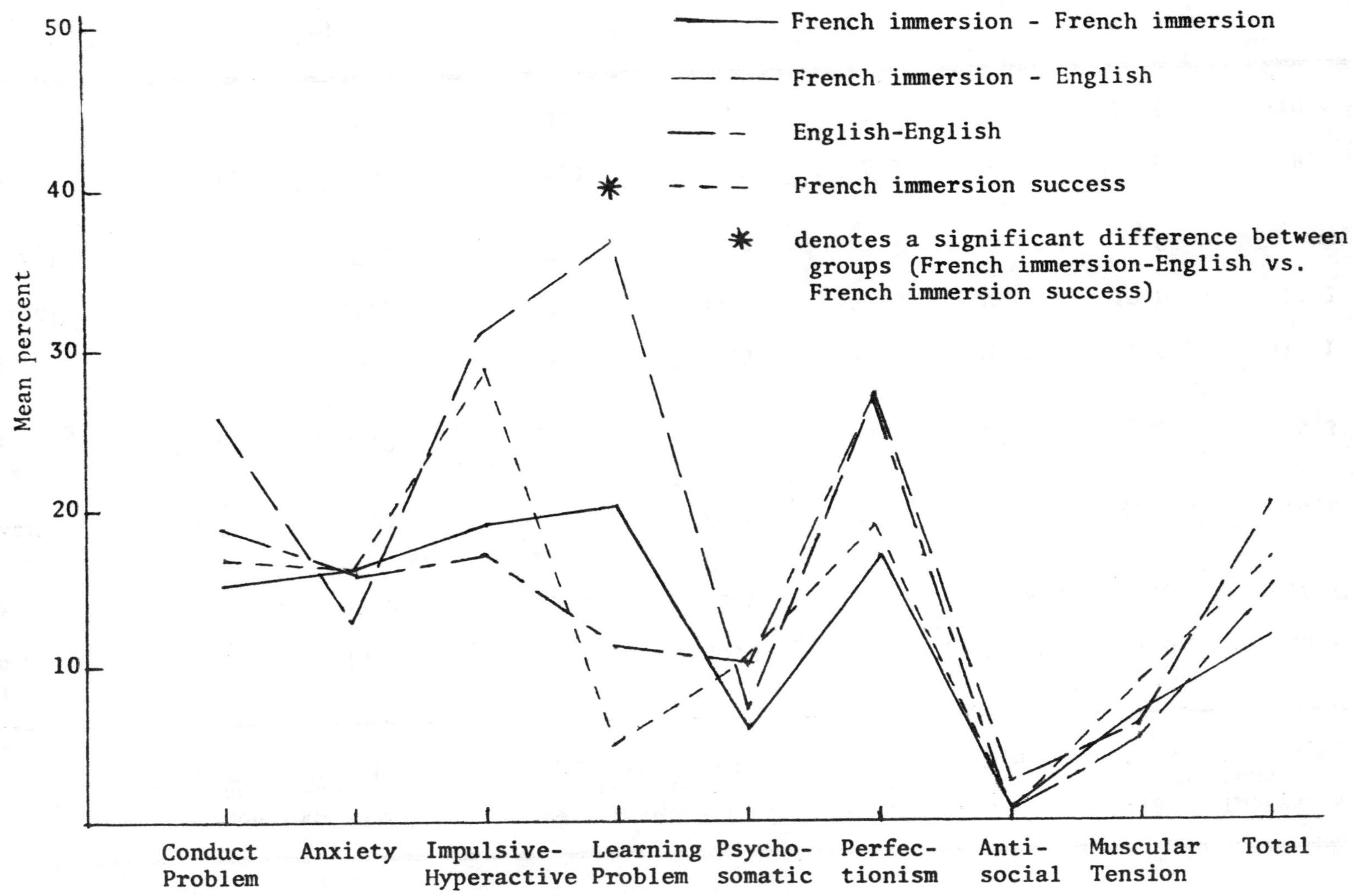

Figure 11: Connors Parent's Symptom Questionnaire ratings of the three French immersion difficulty groups and the French immersion success group at follow-up testing.

TABLE XIX

Mean and Standard Deviation of Percent Scores on the Rating Scales of the Connors Parent's Questionnaire at Follow-up Testing

	French Immersion-French Immersion[1] Mean	S.D.	French Immersion-English[2] Mean	S.D.	English-English[3] Mean	S.D.	French Immersion Success[4] Mean	S.D.
Conduct Problem	15.3	14.4	26.2	14.0	19.7	11.1	17.0	13.1
Anxiety	16.9	17.2	13.5	9.7	16.3	12.6	16.3	16.7
Impulsive-Hyperactive	19.0	20.7	31.8	23.0	17.3	8.5	29.7	24.6
Learning Problem	20.3	23.2	37.5	14.0	11.9	13.5	5.9	9.3
Psycho-somatic	6.7	10.5	7.8	6.5	10.5	12.7	10.5	12.1
Perfectionism	17.3	24.9	27.7	26.0	27.0	26.3	19.0	26.2
Anti-Social	1.8	5.5	2.8	4.3	1.2	3.1	0	0
Muscular Tension	7.4	8.8	6.9	6.3	5.9	6.3	9.5	8.9
Total	12.4	9.1	20.9	8.4	15.6	6.0	17.8	10.4

[1] N=9   [2] N=6   [3] N=7   [4] N=7

examination compared to the French immersion success group (t=4.78, df=8, p<.01). This group also obtained a higher score, although non-significant, on the conduct problem scale, impulsivity-hyperactivity scale, perfectionism scale and total scaled score elevation. It appears that the parents in this group are acutely sensitive to learning and behaviour problems of these children, possibly as a result of the difficulties the child had been having recently in a French immersion program and subsequent switch to an English language program.

2) <u>Connors Teacher's Questionnaire (Appendix 2)</u>

    a) Comparison of the Total French Immersion Difficulty Group and the French Immersion Success Group:

Few Connors Teacher's Questionnaires had been completed at first testing. The results of those obtained at follow-up testing are presented in this section. Figure 12 presents homeroom teacher ratings of the total French immersion difficulty

---

Insert Figure 12 About Here

---

group versus the French immersion success group. The mean ratings and standard deviations of these groups and of the three French immersion difficulty sub-groups are presented in Table XX. The French immersion success group received

---

Insert Table XX About Here

---

substantially lower ratings on all of these scales, which indicates better behaviour. There were significant differences on the scales assessing conduct problem (t=4.07, df=19, p<.01), inattentiveness-passivity (t=4.24, df=8, p<.01),

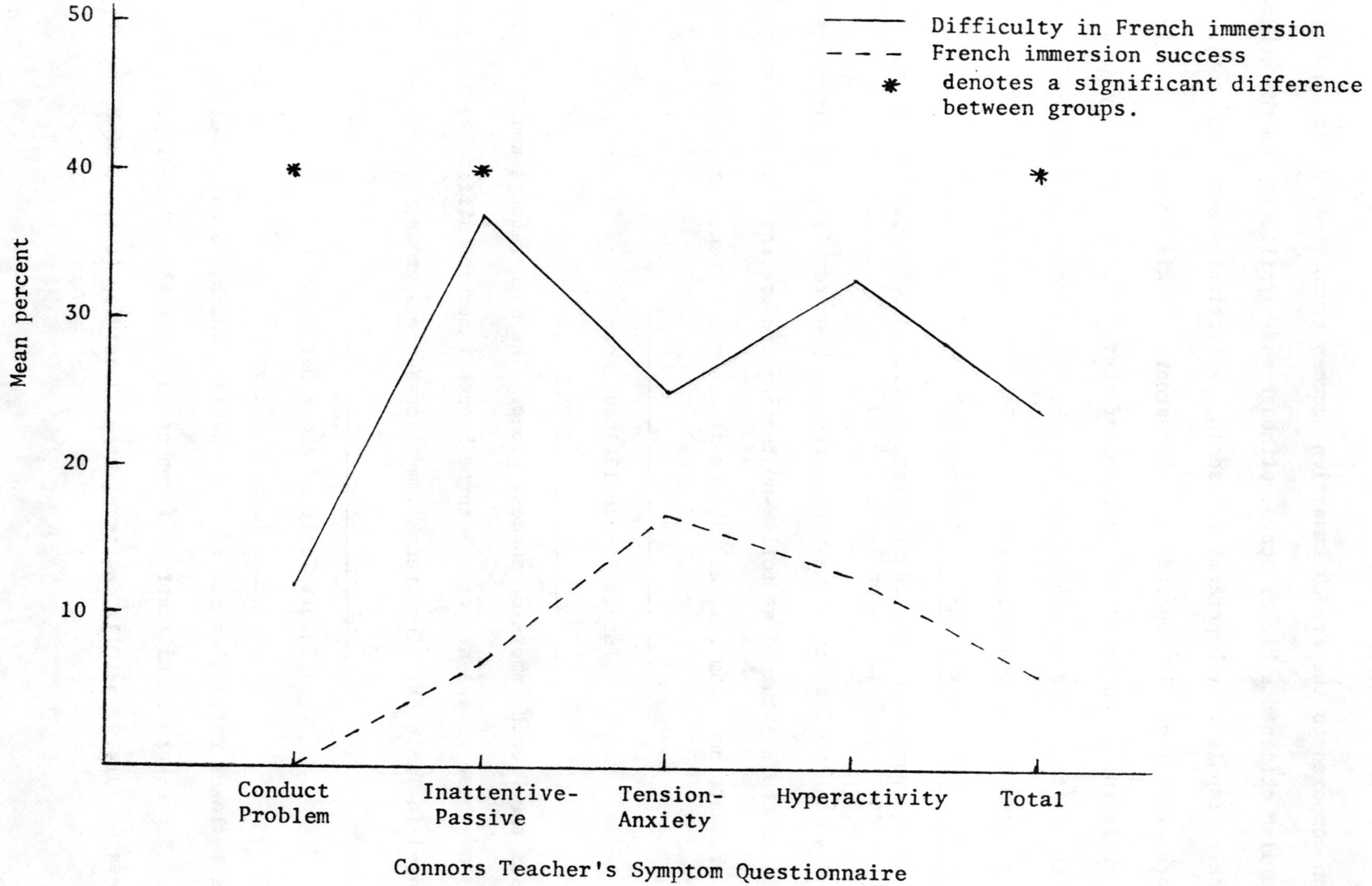

Figure 12: Connors Teacher's Symptom Questionnaire ratings of the total French immersion difficulty group and the French immersion success group at follow-up testing.

TABLE XX

Mean and Standard Deviation of Percent Scores on the Rating Scales of the
Connors Teacher's Questionnaire at Follow-up Testing

		\multicolumn{5}{c}{Connors Rating Scales}
Group		Conduct Problem	Inattentive-Passive	Anxiety	Hyperactivity	Total
Total French Immersion Difficulty[1].	Mean S.D.	12.8 14.0	37.5 22.9	25.1 19.4	33.6 27.2	24.5 14.4
French immersion-French immersion[2].	Mean S.D.	6.9 11.7	38.2 27.9	25.0 19.8	20.8 23.0	18.9 10.6
French immersion-English[3].	Mean S.D.	21.3 13.3	38.9 22.2	31.4 22.2	44.4 31.6	32.7 17.6
English-English[4].	Mean S.D.	12.0 15.4	35.2 20.1	18.9 17.1	39.8 24.9	23.6 13.8
French immersion Success[5].	Mean S.D.	0 0	7.4 8.5	17.8 13.9	13.3 17.6	6.7 4.4

[1]. N=20   [2]. N=8   [3]. N=6   [4]. N=6   [5]. N=3

and total scaled elevation (t=4.34, df=11, p<.05).

    b) Comparison of the three French Immersion Difficulty sub-groups and the French Immersion Success Group:

Figure 13 presents a comparison of the three French immersion difficulty sub-groups versus the French immersion success group on the Connors Teacher's Questionnaire. The three French immersion difficulty groups obtained substantially

---

Insert Figure 13 About Here

---

higher scores on all of the Connors Scales as compared to the French immersion success group. The French immersion difficulty group who had switched to English after first testing obtained significantly higher conduct problem ratings as compared to the French immersion success group (t=3.91, df=5, p<.05). All three French immersion difficulty groups had significantly higher scores on the inattentive-passivity scale and the total sub-scale ratings as compared to the French immersion success group (t=2.79, df=9; t=3.05, df=7; t=2.91, df=7, respectively, p<.05). Thus, teachers were very much aware of inattentiveness and passivity amongst children who had experienced difficulty in French immersion (whether they were now in the French immersion or in the English language program). There was a rather strong tendency generally for the profiles of the French immersion-English switch group and English-English switch groups to resemble each other on the hyperactivity scale, while the French immersion-French immersion difficulty group resembled closely the French immersion success group. It is quite possible that if the child who is having difficulty in French immersion is not a problem insofar as hyperactivity is concerned, his chances are greater of remaining in a French immersion class even if he is not progressing well

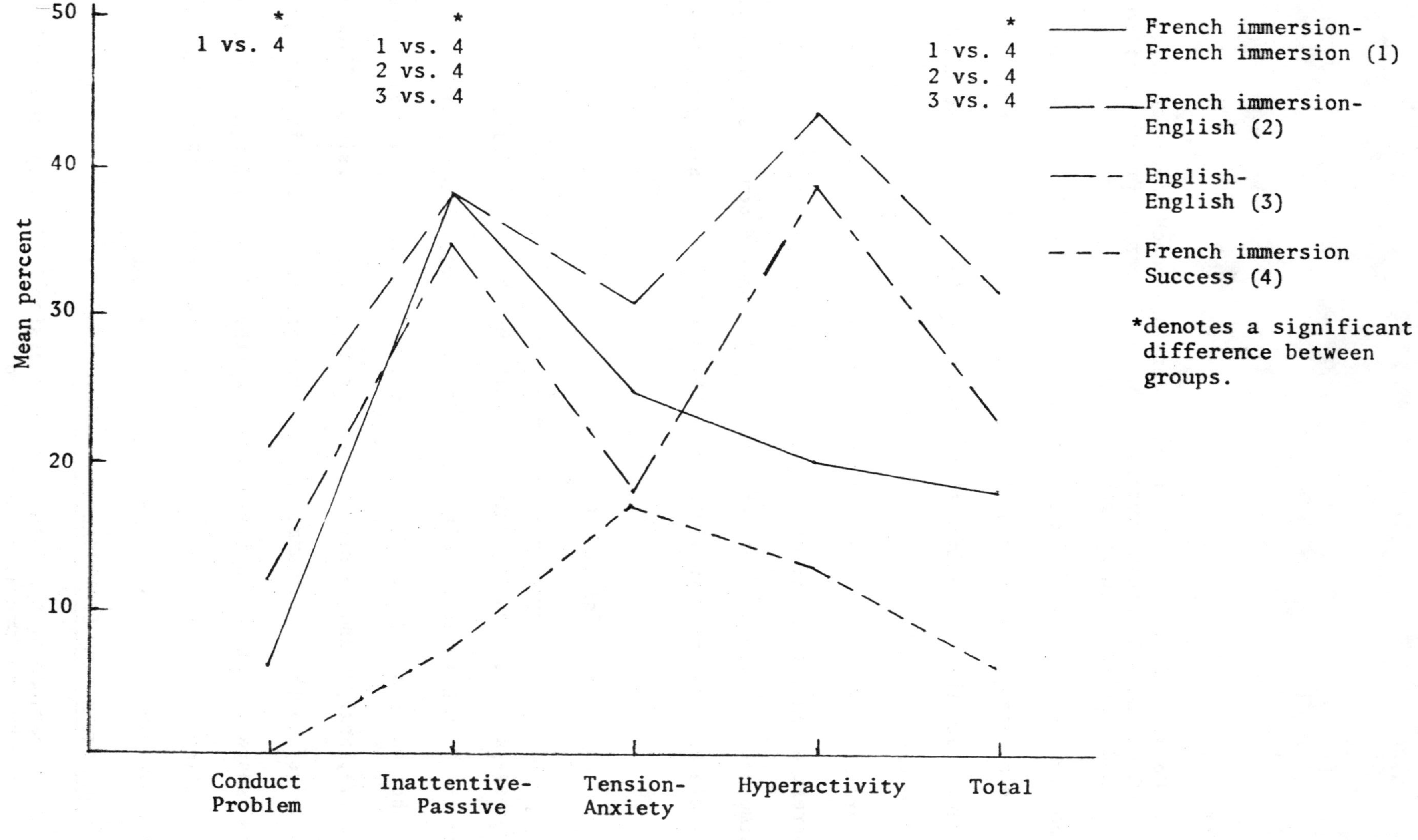

Figure 13: Connors Teacher's Symptom Questionnaire ratings of the three French immersion difficulty groups and the French immersion success group at follow-up testing.

academically.

      c) Connors Ratings of the French immersion-French immersion Difficulty Group and the French immersion Success Group by French immersion and English Language Arts Teachers.

For children in French immersion at the time of follow-up testing (French immersion-French immersion difficulty group and the French immersion success group), both the French immersion teacher and English Language Arts teacher were asked to complete the Connors questionnaire independently. Although these two sets of ratings are available on a very small number of subjects, they are of interest as an indication of the child's behaviour in two different language atmospheres. The mean percent scores and standard deviations on each behaviour scale are presented in Table XXI. The significantly higher ratings on

---

Insert Table XXI About Here

---

inattentiveness-passivity and the total sub-scale by the French immersion teacher for the French immersion difficulty group did not reach significance on the English teacher ratings. However, there was a tendency towards high ratings on the inattentive, anxious and passive scales for the French immersion difficulty group as compared to the French immersion success group. In addition both groups appeared to behave in similar ways regardless of the classroom language with the possible exception of greater anxiety in English class among the French immersion difficulty group. However, this sample was extremely small.

3) Pupil Behaviour Rating Scale (Appendix 2)

      a) Comparison of the Total French Immersion Difficulty Group and the French Immersion Success Group:

This scale has been used as a teacher rating of pupils in French

TABLE XXI

Mean and Standard Deviation of Ratings of the French immersion-French immersion Difficulty Group and the French immersion Success Group by French immersion and English Language Arts Teachers

| Rating Scales | French Immersion Teacher's Ratings ||||| English Teacher's Ratings |||||
| | French Immersion-French Immersion[1] || French Immersion Success[2] || | French Immersion-French Immersion[3] || French Immersion Success[4] || |
	Mean	S.D.	Mean	S.D.	t-prob.	Mean	S.D.	Mean	S.D.	t-prob.
Conduct Problem	6.94	11.7	0	0	.14	4.98	5.4	5.5	3.9	.89
Inattentive-Passive	38.18	27.9	7.4	8.5	.02*	49.99	34.5	11.11	15.7	.11
Anxiety	24.99	19.8	17.77	13.9	.53	35.99	29.66	18.33	2.36	.26
Hyperactivity	20.83	22.95	13.33	17.6	.589	21.09	19.81	21.66	7.07	.96
Total	18.91	10.6	6.69	4.4	.024*	25.57	15.82	15.85	5.87	.29

[1]. N=8   [2]. N=3   [3]. N=5   [4]. N=2

*p<.05

immersion studies (Edwards and Casserly, 1971, 1972, 1973). The mean and standard deviation of teacher ratings of the total French immersion difficulty group and the French immersion success group at follow-up testing are presented in Table XXII. Comparison between these groups, as presented in Figure 14, revealed

---

Insert Table XXII About Here

---

better personal-social behaviour for the French immersion success group.

Insert Figure 14 About Here

---

b) Behaviour Ratings of the French immersion-French immersion Difficulty Group and the French immersion Success Group by French immersion and English Language Arts Teachers:

At follow-up testing, independent ratings by French immersion teachers and English Language Arts teachers were obtained for subjects in the French immersion-French immersion difficulty group and the French immersion success group. The mean ratings and standard deviations are presented in Table XXIII. The

---

Insert Table XXIII About Here

---

results of comparisons of these ratings are presented in Figure 15. There were no

---

Insert Figure 15 About Here

---

significant differences between these groups when rated by either teacher. Once again, the number of subjects involved was quite small.

TABLE XXII

Mean, Standard Deviation and t-probabilities of Pupil Behaviour Ratings of the Total French Immersion Difficulty Group and the French Immersion Success Group at Follow-up Testing

Behaviour Rating Scales	French Immersion Difficulty[1] Mean	S.D.	French Immersion Success[2] Mean	S.D.	t-prob.
Auditory Comprehension	10.5	2.5	11.7	2.5	0.509
Spoken Language	13.4	2.0	12.7	2.3	0.653
Orientation	12.3	2.2	13.7	2.1	0.376
Motor Co-ordination	9.1	2.1	8.7	0.6	0.464
Personal-Social Behaviour	21.1	3.9	25.3	2.1	0.036*
Verbal Total	24.1	4.2	24.3	4.7	0.929
Nonverbal Total	42.3	6.9	47.7	4.2	0.137
Total	66.4	8.8	72.0	8.9	0.382

[1] N=19 [2] N=3
*$p<.05$

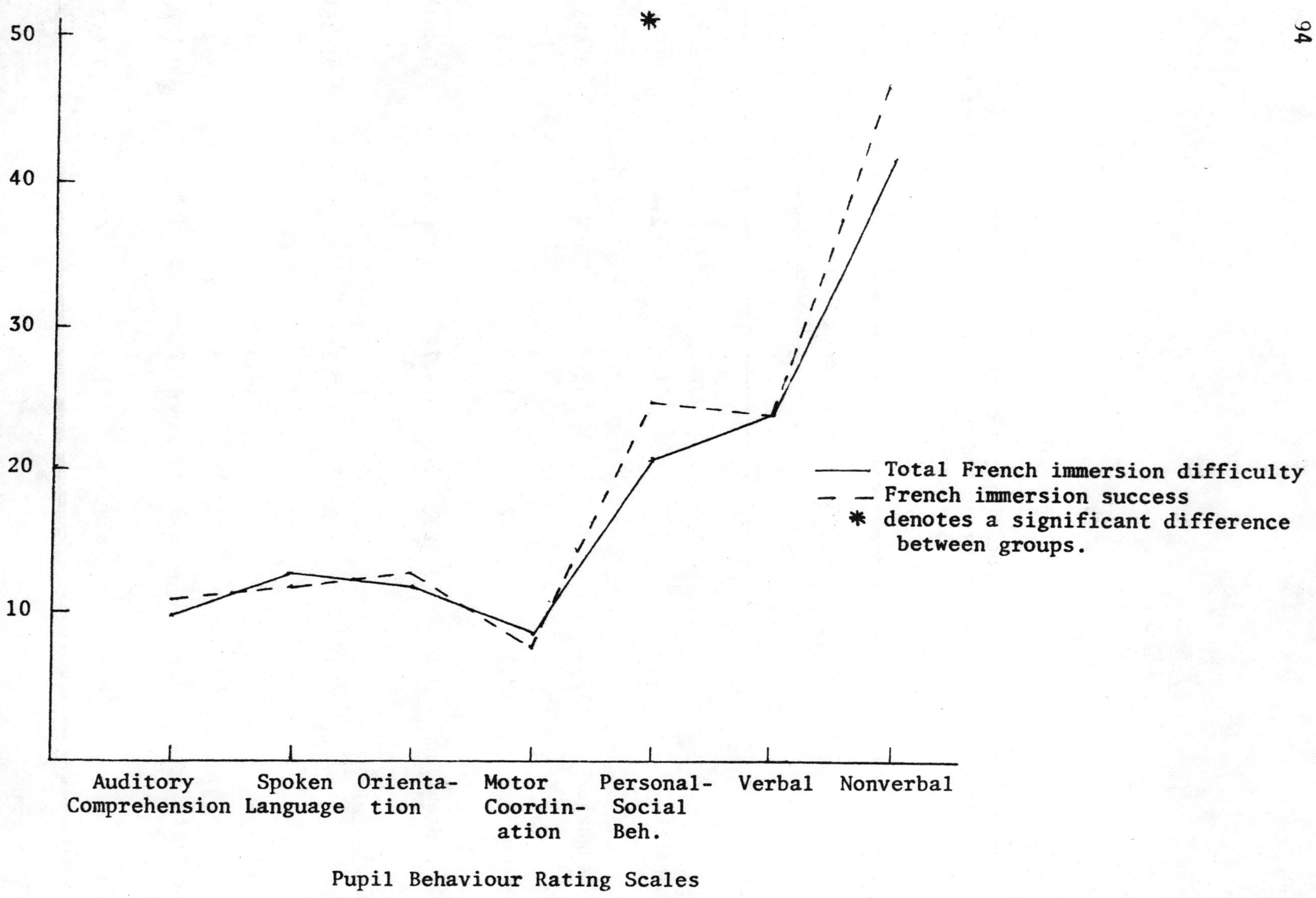

Figure 14: Pupil Behaviour Ratings of the total French immersion difficulty group and the French immersion success group at follow-up testing.

TABLE XXIII

Mean, Standard Deviation and t-probabilities of Pupil Behaviour Ratings by French Immersion and English Language Arts Teachers

	French Immersion Teacher's Ratings						English Language Arts Teacher's Ratings					
	French Immersion[1]		French Immersion Success[2]				French Immersion[3]		French Immersion Success[4]			
	Mean	S.D.	Mean	S.D.	t-prob.		Mean	S.D.	Mean	S.D.	t-prob.	
Auditory Comprehension	9.9	2.2	11.7	2.5	.36		10.3	2.9	14.5	5.0	.462	
Spoken Language	13.0	1.7	12.7	2.3	.834		14.4	3.8	18.5	0.7	.07	
Orientation	13.0	2.8	13.7	2.1	.685		12.7	3.3	13.5	2.1	.706	
Motor Co-ordination	8.7	2.8	8.7	0.6	.939		7.6	.9	8.5	0.7	.295	
Personal-Social Beh.	21.1	4.3	25.3	2.1	.061		20.7	3.6	27.5	7.8	.442	
Verbal	22.9	3.4	24.3	4.7	.658		25.0	6.5	33.0	5.7	.247	
Non-verbal	42.9	8.7	47.7	4.2	.255		41.8	6.3	49.5	10.6	.513	

[1] N=8   [2] N=3   [3] N=6   [4] N=2

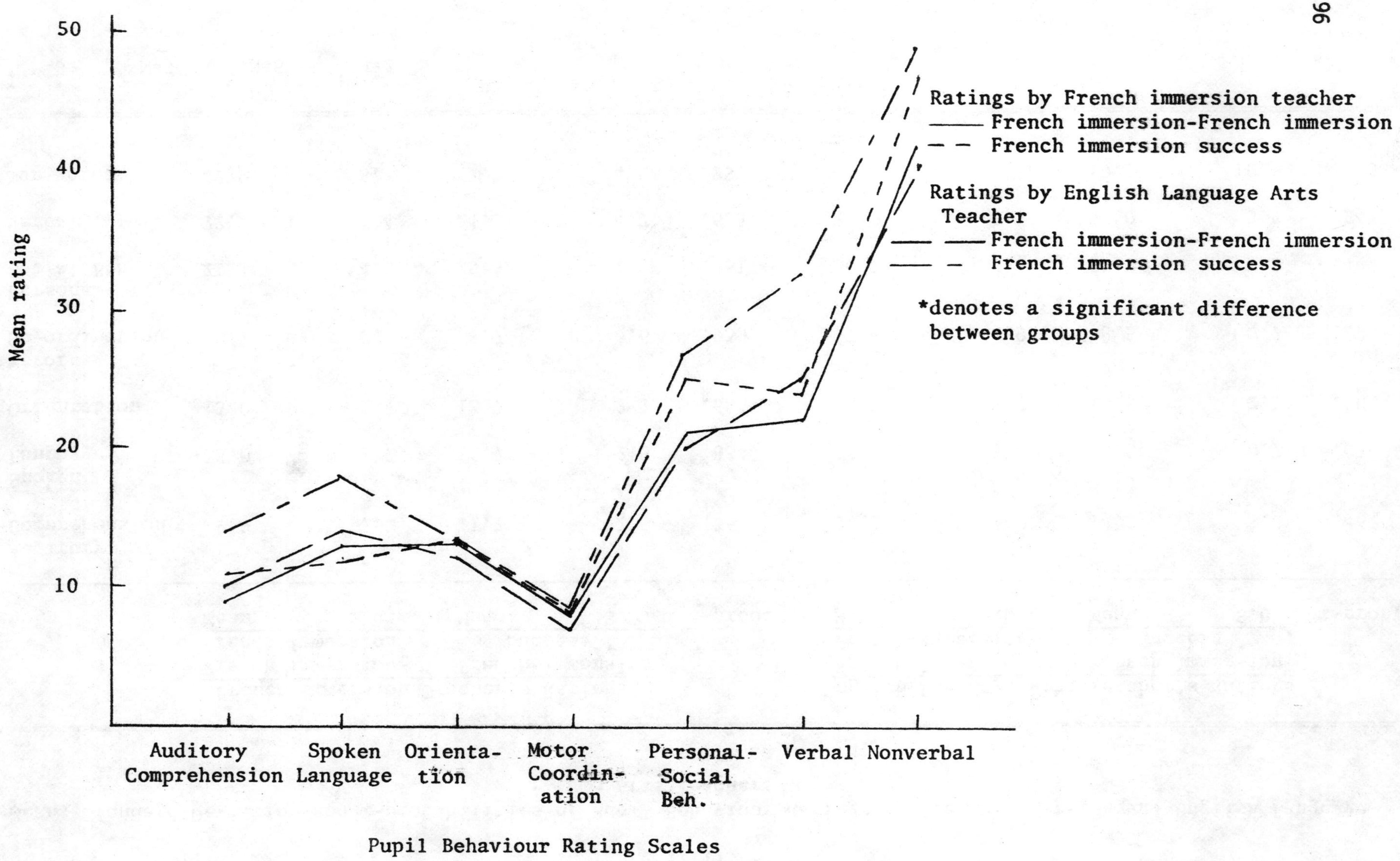

Figure 15: Pupil Behaviour Ratings by French immersion and English Language Arts Teachers.

4) Personality Testing

Some studies of French immersion programming have included objective personality tests in their battery (Edwards and Casserly, 1973; Alexander et al, 1974). The personality test in the present battery included the Children's Personality Questionnaire or the Early School Personality Questionnaire depending on the age of the child. In view of the small numbers, only the profiles for the 12 French immersion difficulty children who received the Early School Personality Questionnaire at first testing will be discussed (Figure 16). This

---

Insert Figure 16 About Here

---

profile would be interpreted clinically as characteristic of an impulsive, enthusiastic, activity-oriented and sociable youngster. These children characteristically are described as coming from secure and affectionate families. It is possible that a child with this personality type would have difficulties functioning effectively and being happy in a highly structured, controlled and more traditionally-oriented program. In view of the small numbers, however, these scores were taken as only preliminary at this time.

5) Amnestic and Attitudinal Information

The questionnaires used for amnestic and attitudinal information are presented in Appendices 2 and 3. The responses by the subject and the parents to the various items were subjected to a Chi-square analysis.

    a) Questions for Subject:

    i) Comparison of the Total French Immersion Difficulty Group and the French Immersion Success Group:

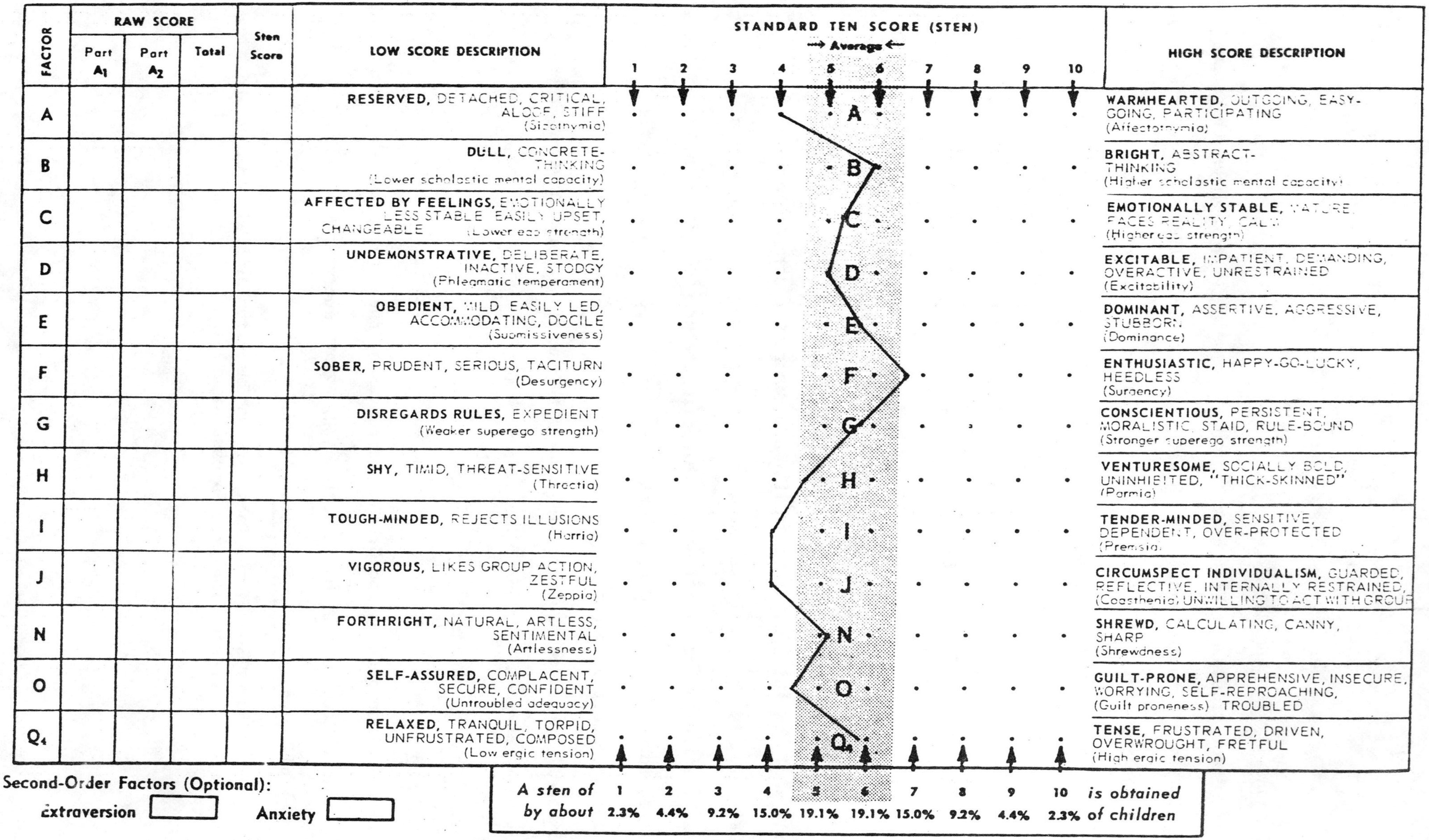

Figure 16: Early School Personality Questionnaire Profile of twelve subjects in the French immersion difficulty group.

On the "Questions for Subject" items there were no significant differences in the responses of the French immersion difficulty group and the French immersion success group.

    ii) Comparison of the Three French Immersion Difficulty Sub-groups and the French Immersion Success Group:

When the French immersion difficulty group was broken down into the three sub-groups as can be seen from Table XXIV, several interesting trends emerged. With regard to question #1, frequency of watching French T.V., only

---

Insert Table XXIV About Here

---

the French immersion-English (33.3%) and the French immersion success group (28.6%) watch French T.V. frequently. A factor which likely contributed substantially to the significant Chi-square was that 42.9% of the French immersion success group do not watch French T.V. at all. With regard to question #4, about fears of family members making fun of the subject speaking French, there was a significant pattern in that 33.3% of the French immersion-English switch group responded "yes", while all other groups responded 100% "no". With regard to question #17, there was a significant trend for both groups of French immersion children who have switched to an English program to like teachers other than their French immersion teacher better.

While there were surprisingly few significant group differences on the "Questions for Subject" items, it was interesting to note that 50% of the French immersion success group speak French to French-speaking children. One third of the French immersion-English switch and 29% of the English-English group, along

TABLE XXIV

Significant Findings for Comparisons Among the Three French Immersion Difficulty Sub-groups and the French Immersion Success Group on Questions for Subject Questionnaire

Question #	Response Code	% Responses French Immersion-French Immersion	French Immersion-English	English-English	French Immersion Success	Chi^2
1.	1.	9.1	50	57.1	42.9	14.68*
	2.	90.1	16.7	42.9	28.6	(df=6)
	3.	0	33.3	0	28.6	
4.	1.	0	33.3	0	0	8.91*
	2.	100	66.7	100	100	(df=3)
17.	1.	9.1	66.7	100	28.6	20.33**
	2.	72.7	33.3	0	28.6	(df=6)
	3.	18.2	0	0	42.9	

*p < .05
**p < .01

with 14% of the French immersion success group expressed the opinion that they do not want to learn to speak French. The French immersion-English switch group and the English-English group were divided in their liking for French immersion, while a majority of the other groups expressed a preference in favour of this program. Thus, it appeared that part of the reason for the French immersion difficulty children remaining in French immersion programming is related to their positive attitudes toward the program.

 b) <u>Family History of Reading Problems</u>

 i) Comparison of the Total French Immersion Difficulty Group and the French Immersion Success Group:

The family history of reading problems questionnaire is presented in Appendix 2. In questioning the parents about the family history of reading and related problems, several trends emerged (see Table XXV). In a comparison of the French immersion difficulty group with the French immersion success group,

---

Insert Table XXV About Here

---

there was a significant tendency for the former group of parents to see their child as having difficulty in learning to read (83% versus 14% respectively), and as being held back in school because of reading difficulty (35% versus 0% respectively). There was also a significant trend for less reading outside of school in the French immersion difficulty group (61% do not read outside school versus 14% in the French immersion success group). Therefore, parents see their French immersion difficulty children as having essentially difficulty in reading, rather than other problems. A total of 36% of the French immersion difficulty siblings had reading problems versus 14% in the French

TABLE XXV

Significant Findings of the Chi^2 Analysis of the Family History of Reading Problems Questionnaire

Question #	Response Code	% Responses French Immersion Difficulty	% Responses French Immersion Success	Chi^2
Subject A	1. Yes	82.6	14.3	13.51**
	2. No	17.4	57.1	(df=2)
	3. Hasn't learned	0	28.6	
Subject B	1. Yes	34.8	0	9.04**
	2. No	65.2	71.4	(df=2)
	3. N/A	0	28.6	
Subject C	1. Yes	34.8	57.1	6.15*
	2. No	60.9	14.3	(df=2)
	3. N/A	4.3	28.6	

Question #	Response Code	French-Immersion French Immersion	French-Immersion English	English-English	French Immersion Success	Chi^2
Grand-parents A	1. Yes	11.1	0	50	0	8.49*
	2. No	88.9	100	50	100	(df=3)
Subject A	1. Yes	70	100	85.7	14.3	15.33*
	2. No	30	0	14.3	57.1	(df=6)
	3. Hasn't learned	0	0	0	28.6	

*p<.05
**p<.01

immersion success group. Therefore, not only are the French immersion difficulty subjects seen as having reading difficulties, but there is a much higher history of reading difficulties in the families of the French immersion difficulty group as compared to the French immersion success group.

    ii) Comparison of the Three French Immersion Difficulty Sub-groups and the French Immersion Success Group:

Comparisons among the three French immersion difficulty sub-groups and the French immersion success group indicated that children in all three difficulty groups had a problem learning to read, especially those who switched to English between testings. In addition, this same group had a significantly greater incidence of reading problems among maternal grandparents (see Table XXV).

There were some other interesting but non-significant trends. When the switch groups were combined, they tended to have more siblings with a reading problem (41.7%) and more fathers with a reading problem (15.4%) than did the difficulty group who remained in French immersion (30% and 0% respectively). In addition, more children who switched to English were held back in school due to reading problems (46.2%) than were those who remained in the French immersion program (11%).

    c) Background Information

A third source of amnestic and attitudinal information was a questionnaire titled "Background Information" (Appendix 3) which was completed during an interview with the parents at the time of follow-up testing. Once again Chi-square analyses were performed on the frequency scores.

    i) Comparison of the Total French Immersion Difficulty Group and the French Immersion Success Group:

The significant differences found in this analysis are presented in Table XXVI. Significantly more parents in the French immersion success group (71%)

Insert Table XXVI About Here

---

have taken French courses compared to the French immersion difficulty group, (29%) (Parents #4). There was a high percentage of favourable attitudes towards the course taken in the French immersion success group (Parents #5). Few subjects in the French immersion success group had been exposed to teachers other than a French immersion teacher and they tended to like this teacher. Many (79.2%) of the French immersion difficulty parents also reported that their children did not get along better with other teachers than with the French immersion teacher (School #14). A great many more parents in the French immersion success group (42.9%) saw their children as good readers in French versus only 4.2% of the French immersion difficulty group (School #10). In addition, although non-significant, 42% of the French immersion difficulty parents also described their children as poor readers in English while none of the children in the French immersion success group were described as poor readers in English (School #12).

Several other non-significant trends were of interest. Twelve and a half percent of the French immersion difficulty group versus 29% of the French immersion success group claimed that some French was spoken at home (Parents #1). There was a favourable attitude amongst all parents (only one parent in the French immersion success group excepted) in wanting their children to learn to speak French (Parents #8). The parents in the French immersion success group, particularly, encouraged their

TABLE XXVI

Significant Findings in the Chi^2 Analysis of the Background Information Questionnaire comparing the Total French Immersion Difficulty Group and the French Immersion Success Group

Question #	Response Code	% Responses French Immersion Difficulty	% Responses French Immersion Success	Chi^2
Parents #4	1	4.2	28.6	8.12*
	2	25	42.9	(df=3)
	3	16.7	28.6	
	4	54.2	0	
Parents #5	1	25	71.4	7.96*
	2	4.2	14.3	(df=3)
	3	0	0	
	4	16.7	14.3	
	5	54.2	0	
School #10	1	4.2	42.9	9.5 *
	2	20.8	14.3	(df=3)
	3	41.7	0	
	4	0	0	
	5	33.3	42.9	
School #14	1	16.7	14.3	7.3 *
	2	79.2	42.9	(df=2)
	3	4.2	42.9	

*$p < .05$

children to watch French television (71% versus 43%) (Parents #11).

Gardner and Lambert (1959) have discussed instrumental and integrative orientations toward second language learning. In the instrumental orientation, utilitarian or practical aspects of learning a second language are considered important, e.g. enhanced career opportunities. In the integrative orientation the aim of second language learning is to communicate with, interact with, or to become in some small way a part of the other language community (Gardner, 1974). High school students who had an integrative orientation tended to have greater success in second language learning than those with instrumental orientations. French immersion difficulty parents and French immersion success parents tended to cite instrumental reasons for the importance of learning French (45.8% and 42.9% respectively) or some combination of instrumental and integrative reasons (37.5% and 42.9%, respectively) (Parents #9). This tendency was also observed in the reasons cited for enrolling a child in French immersion (Parents #13). However, the French immersion success parents tended to cite more integrative reasons, either alone or in combination with instrumental reasons (14.3% versus 4.2% integrative and 42.9% versus 33.3% both integrative and instrumental).

Since it is possible that being bussed to a school in order to receive French immersion programming may have a negative effect on the progress of some children, it was interesting to note that a higher percentage (42%) of the French immersion difficulty group were not in a neighbourhood school versus 29% in the French immersion success group (Community #27). A great many of the parents (42% of the French immersion difficulty group and 14% of the French immersion success group) worried about how successful their children would be in learning regular school subjects through French (School #15) and many (83% of the French immersion difficulty group and 43% of the French immersion success group) have considered removing the child from French immersion (School #17). However, a much smaller number actually regret enrolling their child in a French immersion program (29% of the French immersion difficulty group and 14% of the French immersion success group) (School #19). One half of the French immersion difficulty parents and 71.4% of the French immersion success parents were satisifed with their child's progress in learning French in the French immersion program (School #5).

In terms of transferring out of a French immersion program, this was suggested in 50% of the French immersion difficulty group and 29% of the French immersion success group (School #25). The reasons most frequently given were difficulty in learning (58% in the French immersion difficulty group and zero percent in the French immersion success group); behaviour problems (33% in the French immersion difficulty group and 100% in the French immersion success group); and emotional problems (8% in the French immersion difficulty group and zero percent in the French immersion success group). When a switch was actually made, this was done on the insistence of school authorities in only one case and, usually, was done by parents in consultation with the school (61.5%). The parents summarized the reasons for their child's difficulty as: a learning problem (61%), behaviour problems (23%), emotional problems (7%), and no progress (7%). Following a switch into an English language program, 61.5% of the parents were satisfied with their child's progress in that program.

  ii) Comparison of the three French Immersion Difficulty Sub-groups and the French Immersion Success Group:

The French immersion difficulty group was broken down into group A -

French immersion on both testings; group B - French immersion on first testing, English programming on second testing; and, group C - English programming on both testings. Group D is the French immersion success group. The significant Chi-squares obtained on several of the "Background Information" questionnaire items are presented in Table XXVII. Groups A and D reported a very high percentage of

---

Insert Table XXVII About Here

---

friendships in the French immersion class (Community #26). In addition, the children in group B, who were in an English program at follow-up testing, reported that their friends were still in French immersion while many children in group C had made new friends in the English program.

In terms of the parents' attitude towards French immersion and feelings about enrolling another child in this program, 100% of the parents of the French immersion children who were having difficulty but were continuing in the program (group A) would enroll another child while only 66% of group B parents and 43% of group C parents would do so (School #20). In the French immersion success group (group D), 85% would enrol another child in French immersion. Therefore, those parents who had switched their child to an English program were more split on this question, many not wishing to enrol another child. These same parents considered that their child had a strong dislike for French immersion (83% of group B and 86% of group C), whereas 80% of group A and 86% of group D considered that their child had a good feeling about French immersion (School #21). Sixty-seven percent of the group B parents and 100% of the group C parents claimed that their child had a positive

TABLE XXVII

Significant Findings in the Chi^2 Analysis of the Background Information Questionnaire for the Three French Immersion Difficulty Sub-groups and the French Immersion Success Group

Question #	Response Code	% Responses French immersion-French immersion (A)	French immersion-English (B)	English-English (C)	French immersion Success (D)	Chi^2
Community #26	1	90.9	100	42.9	100	11.6**
	2	9.1	0	57.1	0	(df=3)
School #20	1	100	66.7	42.9	85.7	8.7*
	2	0	33.3	57.1	14.3	(df=3)
School #21	1	80	16.7	14.3	85.7	13.3**
	2	20	83.3	85.7	14.3	(df=3)
School #22	1	12.5	66.7	100	16.7	25.8**
	2	0	33.3	0	0	(df=6)
	10	87.5	0	0	83.3	

*p<.05
**p<.01

attitude toward the English language program (School #22).

Several non-significant but interesting trends emerged. There were sub-groups (group B, and group D) who reported an equally high percentage of French in the family (33% in group B and 29% in group D) (Parents #1). Therefore, it would appear that for children in group B, having French in the home did not prevent the difficulty experienced in French immersion. There was a higher percentage of parents in groups A and D who themselves would like to learn French (54.5% and 43% respectively) versus the parents of children who have switched to English (16.7% of group B parents and 28.6% of group C parents) (Parents #3).

When asked why it was important to learn to speak French (Parents #9), group C parents cited instrumental reasons most often (71%) followed by group D (42.9%). Group A and B parents cited both instrumental and integrative reasons (46% and 50% respectively) more often than solely instrumental reasons (36% and 33% respectively). These trends were again found for parents' reasons for enrolling their child in French immersion (Parents #13).

The parents of the group B children found that their children were not learning to read French (67%) (School #9), claim that the children had difficulty in reading in English as well (50%) (School #12), and felt that their children were not getting along with the French immersion teacher (50%) (School #13). In general, parents of children who had switched to English (groups B and C) expressed a higher concern about these issues and were particularly worried about the success of their children in learning subjects other than French (50% and 71.4% respectively) (School #15). The parents of all groups reported that they have considered removing their child from French immersion (73% in group A, 83% in group B and 100% in group C, 43% in group D) (School #17). However, when asked how many regret that their children have been enrolled in French immersion the percentages were smaller (18% in group A, 33% in group B, 43% in group C and 14% in group D) (School #18). Groups B and D tended to have more siblings in French immersion (50% and 57.1% respectively) versus groups A and C (36.4% and 14.3% respectively) (Siblings #16). More parents of children who had switched to English (groups B and C) tended to feel that a transfer to the English program would not upset their child's social relationships (83.3 and 85.7% respectively versus 54.5 and 57.1% for groups A and D) (Community #28). Children who have switched to English (groups B and C) were judged to have a poor understanding of French by their parents (50 and 42.9%) as compared to groups A and D who were still in French immersion (18.2 and 14.3% respectively) (School #6).

Parents' ratings of their child's behaviour in French immersion and in the English class or program were classified as enthusiastic, shy and withdrawn, behaviour problem or no complaints (School #23, #24). Groups B and C tended to be shy and withdrawn in French immersion (45.5% and 33.3% respectively) but not in English class (both zero percent). Group A tended towards shyness in both French immersion (45.5%) and in English class (33.3%). The French immersion success group was not described as shy, but this group was frequently rated as a behaviour problem in both French immersion (42.9%) and in English class (25%). Group B was also described as a behaviour problem in French immersion (50%) and in English class (33.3%). Very few children were described as enthusiastic in French immersion (9.1% in group A, zero percent in groups B and C and 14.3% in group D). Enthusiastic behaviour was more evident in English classes (11.1% in group A, 33.3% in group B, 42.9% in group C and 25% in group D). Thus, the children who have switched to English (groups B and C) are now in a program in which they are less shy, exhibit fewer behaviour problems and are more enthusiastic.

iii) A comparison of the French immersion difficulty children who have remained in French immersion versus the two groups of French immersion difficulty children who have switched to English:

The significant Chi-squares found in this analysis are presented in Table XXVIII. There was a significantly higher percentage of children who have

---
Insert Table XXVIII About Here
---

switched to English whose language of beginning reading instruction was English (zero percent in the French immersion group still in French immersion and 46% in the English switch group) (School #8). In terms of the parents' attitude toward enrolling other children in French immersion, 100% of the parents of children still in French immersion would enroll another child versus 54% of the parents of the switch group (School #20). Eighty percent of the parents of the difficulty group still in French immersion claimed that their child liked French immersion whereas only 15% of the switch group children liked it (School #21). Once the child had switched, 85% appeared to have liked the English program (School #22).

Several non-significant but interesting trends emerged. More parents of the French immersion difficulty group still in French immersion, encouraged the children to speak French at home (64% versus 38% in the switch group) (Parents #12). Parents of children who have switched to English most often cited instrumental reasons for the importance of learning to speak French (53.8% versus 36.4% of parents of children still in French immersion) (Parents # 9). The latter group of parents tended to cite a combination of instrumental and integrative reasons most often (45.5% versus 30.8% of the switch group parents). These trends were also observed in the reasons for enrolling the subject in French immersion (Parents #13). There

TABLE XXVIII

Significant Findings in the Chi^2 Analysis of the Background Information Questionnaire for the Comparison of the French immersion-French immersion Difficulty Group and the Two Groups who have switched to English

Question #	Response Code	% Responses French immersion-French immersion	Switches	Chi^2
School #8	1	0	46.2	4.1*
	2	100	53.8	(df=1)
School #20	1	100	53.8	4.5*
	2	0	46.2	(df=1)
School #21	1	80	15.4	7.2**
	2	20	84.6	(df=1)
School #22	1	12.5	84.6	17.1**
	2	0	15.4	(df=2)
	10	87.5	0	

*p<.05
**p<.01

appeared to be no differences in the incidence of siblings also in French immersion (36% in the French immersion group versus 31% in the switch group) (Siblings #16), however, more of the switches appear to have French-speaking friends (36% versus 69% of children still in French immersion) (Community #25). It was interesting that many more parents of the French immersion difficulty children who continued in French immersion felt that a switch to English would upset their child's social relationships (46% versus 15% of switches) (Community #28). There was a much higher incidence of reporting that the subject did not get along with the French immersion teacher in the switch group (38% versus 9% of those still in French immersion) (School #13).

The parents of the children who switched were very worried about the subject's progress in subjects other than French (62% versus 18% of parents of children still in French immersion) (School #15) and regret having sent their child to French immersion (38% versus 18%) (School #19). Parents in both groups were split on the question of satisfaction with their child's progress in learning French. Fifty-four percent of parents of children still in French immersion and 46.2% of parents of children who had switched were satisfied while 45.5% versus 53.8% were dissatisfied. More of the switches were poor readers in both French (46.2% versus 36.4% of children still in French immersion) and English (53.8% versus 36.4% of children still in French immersion) (School #10, #12).

In terms of behaviour in French immersion and in English class (School #23, 24), none of the switches were enthusiastic in French immersion but they were much more enthusiastic in English class (38.5%), whereas many children in both groups were shy in French immersion (45.5% of switches and 30.8% of children still in French immersion), fewer were shy in English class (33.3% and zero percent respectively). None of the children who remained in French immersion were behaviour problems in this class while 38.5% of switches had been a behaviour problem in French immersion.

FOLLOW-UP ASSESSMENT: PSYCHOMETRIC AND ACADEMIC ACHIEVEMENT TESTS

As was mentioned earlier, 24 subjects were brought in for follow-up testing. Not all subjects were brought in for retesting since there was insufficient test-retest interval in some cases, one family did not wish to participate and three could not be located. Of the 24 who were brought in for retesting the Wechsler Intelligence Scale for Children was not administered to four because of a short test-retest interval. For comparison purposes, seven of the eight subjects in the French immersion success group were brought in for follow-up testing. One of the seven children, even though doing very well in a French immersion program, experienced severe emotional disturbance, seemingly unrelated to school activity and had been removed from French immersion four months prior to follow-up testing after fifteen months in a French immersion program.

The French immersion difficulty group was subdivided into three groups: those who were in French immersion at both testings (French immersion-French immersion); those who had switched to an English program between testings (French-immersion-English); and those who had experienced difficulty in French immersion but were in an English program at both testings (English-English). The time in French immersion, time in English for subjects who had been switched, reasons for transferring to English, school boards, and the test-retest interval for the three French immersion difficulty sub-groups and the French immersion success group are presented in Table XXIX.

Table XXIX About Here

TABLE XXIX

Descriptive Information at Follow-up Testing

Groups by School Situation:	First Testing Retesting	French Immersion French Immersion	French Immersion English	English English	French Immersion Success Group
Number of Children		11	7	6	7
Time in French Immersion	Mean S.D.	27.9 months 14.6	18.7 months 10.8	13.8 months 10.6	22.8 months 14.5
Time in English since Transfer	Mean S.D.	0 months 0	12.7 months 6.250	27.1 months 12.7	4 months
Reasons[1]. For Transfer to English	Learning difficulty Behaviour Problem Emotional Problem No French Immersion available		5,1 1,1 1	4,2 1 1,1	1 1
School Boards	Ottawa Separate Carleton Separate Ottawa Carleton	 7 4	1 2 1 3	2 2 2	 6 1
Test-retest Interval		1.2 years	1.8 years	1.4 years	1.0 years

[1] Underlined frequencies refer to secondary reasons. Other frequencies are primary reasons.

As can be seen from this table, the time in French immersion was noticeably longer for the French immersion-French immersion group and the French immersion success group. The reason for switching to an English program for the French immersion-English group and the English-English group was overwhelmingly reported as difficulty in learning. The interval between first testing and retest was 1.4 years for the total French immersion difficulty group which could be broken down for the three French immersion difficulty sub-groups as is shown in Table XXIX. By comparison the test-retest interval for the French immersion success group was 1.0 years.

An attenuated test battery was administered on second testing. Various rating scales were completed, including the Connors Questionnaires for parents and teachers, family history of reading problems and two questionnaires especially designed for this study, which have already been discussed. The tests administered included the Wechsler Intelligence Scale for Children, Peabody Picture Vocabulary Test, Wide Range Achievement Test for reading, spelling and arithmetic and the Test de Rendement en Français.

ANALYSIS AND RESULTS

1) <u>French Immersion Difficulty Group Versus French Immersion Success Group</u>

Levels of performance of children who had difficulty in French immersion and children who were successful in French immersion were compared at first testing and follow-up testing by means of t-tests. Table XXX presents the means, standard

---

Table XXX About Here

TABLE XXX

Mean, Standard Deviation and t-probability of Significant Differences Between the French Immersion Difficulty Group and the French Immersion Success Group at First Testing and at Follow-up Testing

Test	French Immersion Difficulty Group Mean	S.D.	French Immersion Success Group Mean	S.D.	t-prob.
WISCVIQ	100.9	11.6	108.4	8.1	0.050
WRAT:					
Reading	94.3	10.6	120.4	17.9	0.00
Spelling	91.8	11.2	109.7	16.9	0.019
Arithmetic	97.6	10.0	106.2	9.1	0.016
ITPA:					
VISRECS	36.2	4.9	43.0	3.4	0.013
AUDMEMS	36.8	6.2	43.2	3.9	0.034
KNOXMA	7.9	2.4	10.9	3.9	0.012
KNOXMEMQ	110.3	21.4	152.7	41.6	0.00
ESPQ G	5.9	2.2	3.3	0.6	0.003
ESPQ J	3.9	2.6	8.3	1.5	0.009
CPQ D	5.0	1.1	8.3	1.5	0.034
Connors Teacher:					
Conduct Problem	23.5	23.4	4.2	5.9	0.04
Inattentive-Passive	43.5	32.2	5.5	7.8	0.008
Second testing					
WRAT:					
Reading	93.4	13.8	110.6	15.3	0.028
Spelling	85.6	17.6	108.0	17.6	0.016
Arithmetic	89.8	17.1	105.3	8.3	0.004
Pupil Behaviour Rating:					
Personal-Social	21.1	3.9	25.3	2.1	0.036
Connors Parent:					
Learning Problem	22.3	20.1	5.9	9.3	0.007
Connors Teacher:					
Conduct Problem	12.8	14.0	0.0	0.0	0.001
Inattentive-Passive	37.5	22.9	7.4	8.5	0.003
Total	24.4	14.4	6.7	4.4	0.001

deviations and t-probabilities for tests on which there were significant differences between the French immersion difficulty group and the French immersion success group. It can be seen that the group described as experiencing success in the French immersion program had higher scores on Verbal IQ, academic achievement test for reading, spelling and arithmetic, certain visual and auditory tests from the Illinois Test of Psycholinguistic Abilities, higher visual attention span and were described as having better performance levels on tests of adjustment. These same trends on academic achievement tests and tests of adjustment were maintained on re-examination 1.4 years later for the French immersion difficulty group and 1.0 years later for the French immersion success group.

2) <u>The Three French Immersion Difficulty Sub-groups versus the French Immersion Success Group</u>

      a) Comparison of Difference Scores on the WISC Verbal IQ, WISC Performance IQ, Peabody IQ and Wide Range Achievement Tests:

Difference scores were calculated between test scores on first testing and follow-up testing by subtracting the score at second testing from that obtained on first testing for each subject. The difference scores on the WISC Verbal IQ, WISC Performance IQ, Peabody IQ and Wide Range Achievement Test scaled scores for reading, spelling and arithmetic were subjected to one-way analyses of variance with the three French immersion difficulty sub-groups and the French immersion success group as the independent variable. The means, standard deviations, difference scores and results of the analyses of variance are presented in Table XXXI. There were no significant

---

Table XXXI About Here

TABLE XXXI

Mean, Standard Deviation and Mean Difference Score and ANOVA Results for Selected Measures at First Testing and Retesting for the Four Comparison Groups

Tests	French Immersion-French Immersion Mean	S.D.	Diff. Score	French Immersion-English Mean	S.D.	Diff. Score	English-English Mean	S.D.	Diff. Score	French Immersion Success Mean	S.D.	Diff. Score	ANOVA Results F-ratio	df Score
WISCVIQ														
First testing	107.0	11.8	0.18	99.8	10.3	1.33	100.4	9.4	-2.43	108.9	8.1	-4.5	0.838	3,28
Retesting	108.25	12.4		98.5	8.8		102.5	6.8		111.4	8.7			
WISCPIQ														
First testing	108.2	10.9	1.46	110.8	3.9	-2.33	110.1	11.9	2.7	108.6	8.2	-0.13	0.865	3,28
Retesting	109.8	8.8		113.2	7.0		104.5	9.6		109.9	9.6			
PEABIQ														
First testing	110.0	12.9	1.4	98.8	11.3	-1.6	103.2	5.1	-4.0	106.7	11.4	2.4	0.660	3,25
Retesting	108.6	10.0		101.5	10.8		108.0	5.9		104.3	15.2			
WRARSS														
First Testing	96.0	9.5	4	93.3	9.2	-3.5	89.0	9.9	-5.0	120.4	17.9	6.7	1.615	3,28
Retesting	90.8	14.4		94.0	13.7		94.0	13.7		110.6	15.4			
WRASSS														
First Testing	91.9	6.9	10	91.2	5.7	-3.0	88.7	11.6	1.0	109.8	16.9	2.6	0.841	3,28
Retesting	78.7	21.0		87.5	8.9		87.5	8.9		108.0	17.6			
WRAASS														
First Testing	99.8	8.3	11.73	98.2	8.4	5.17	95.1	8.5	0.0	106.2	9.1	1.7	1.229	3,28
Retesting	84.4	24.4		94.5	5.3		94.5	5.0		105.3	8.3			

differences between the four groups when the differences between first and second testing were compared for WISCVIQ (F=0.838, df=3,28, p>.05), and WISCPIQ (F=0.865, df=3,28, p>.05).

With regard to academic achievement levels, there were no significant differences in reading among the difference scores of the four sub-groups (F=1.615, df=3,28, p>.05), spelling (F=0.841, df=3,28, p>.05) or arithmetic (F=1.229, df=3,28, p>.05). Although the differences were not significant the subjects who had switched to English (French immersion-English group and English-English group) showed improvement in reading at second testing, while this was not apparent in the two groups who were still in French immersion. Children having difficulty in French immersion and who were still in a French immersion program at second testing showed the greatest relative lag in English reading and spelling skills.

In addition, the analysis of variance performed on difference scores for the Peabody Picture Vocabulary IQ measure failed to reveal any significant differences among the four comparison groups. However, the French immersion success group and the French immersion-French immersion group showed a slight loss in vocabulary development as measured by the Peabody IQ score. The two groups who had switched to English programs made slight gains over the test-retest interval. This finding is consistent with the academic achievement test results. The retardation is receptive vocabulary development for children in the French immersion-French immersion group is difficult to explain at this time, but will be monitored very carefully in our further follow-up study. This finding is of considerable interest since it fits in with other findings which indicate that this French immersion-French immersion difficulty group seems to suffer in comparison to the subjects who switched to an English language program. However, the findings are most tentative at the present time.

b) PEABODY PICTURE VOCABULARY TEST: Mental Age Scores and Receptive versus Reading Vocabulary:

The Peabody Picture Vocabulary Test results for first testing and follow-up testing for all groups are presented in Appendix 7. Scores on the Peabody Test can be converted to Mental Age (MA) scores. One may consider that the Peabody MA is equal to or greater than chronological age (CA) in children who have good vocabulary. The frequencies and percentages of subjects with good and poor vocabularies in each group are presented in Table 1 of Appendix 7. Children in English at both testings had the best vocabularies at both testings while those who switched to English between testings showed the most noticeable improvement in vocabulary development. For the French immersion success group the percent of subjects with good vocabularies actually decreased from first to second testing.

In terms of mean MA at first and second testing, presented in Table 2 of Appendix 7, all groups showed some improvement in vocabulary development and this improvement was most noticeable in the two groups who had switched to an English language program. Thus, the children who were in the English language program showed the greatest acceleration in vocabulary development.

The Peabody Picture Vocabulary Test requires that the subject listen to a word and point to a corresponding picture from a multiple choice display. This measure is characteristically used as a test of receptive vocabulary. This test has two forms (A and B) in our Laboratory. Form B is administered in the standard fashion but Form A is given in a novel fashion in that the subject must read the word and point to the corresponding picture. Thus, the discrepancy score between Form B and Form A gives an index of the difference between the subject's receptive vocabulary and reading vocabulary. These scores at first testing and retesting for the four comparison groups are presented in Table 3 of Appendix 7. In terms of form B minus A discrepancies, the French immersion difficulty groups had the highest discrepancy at both first and second testing, however, this discrepancy was smaller at second testing which may indicate a tendency toward improvement in reading vocabulary.

c) Wide Range Achievement Test: Analysis of Discrepancy Scores:

Two types of discrepancy scores were calculated on the academic achievement tests: first, the discrepancy between achievement score obtained and the actual class level of the child; and, secondly, the discrepancy between the achievement score obtained and the score expected on the basis of the child's age. These discrepancies may be different in an individual case. For example, a child may be in grade two having failed a grade. If he is just beginning grade two for the second time and his reading score is 2.0, the discrepancy between achievement score obtained and actual grade placement would be zero, whereas there would be a one grade discrepancy between the actual achievement score and his expected level based on age. The discrepancy scores for each individual subject at first testing and follow-up testing on the academic achievement tests are presented in Appendix 8.

i) Mean Discrepancy Scores:

The mean discrepancy scores in reading, spelling and arithmetic for actual and expected grade levels at first testing for the total sample of 32 subjects are presented in Table XXXII. In the French immersion difficulty group, the 10 subjects

---

Table XXXII About Here

TABLE XXXII

Mean WRAT Discrepancy Scores[1] for Actual and Expected Grade Levels for all Subjects at First Testing

	All Subjects at First Testing		
Test	French Immersion Difficulty		French Immersion Success
	In French Immersion- 1st Testing	In English- 1st Testing	
Reading:			
Actual	.22	.41	-1.61
Expected	.48	.81	-1.75
Spelling:			
Actual	.36	.64	- .66
Expected	.6	1.04	- .78
Arithmetic:			
Actual	- .01	.18	- .31
Expected	.23	.58	- .44

[1] A positive discrepancy score indicates that the achievement score was below actual or expected grade level.

A negative discrepancy score indicates that the achievement score was above the actual or expected grade level.

who were in English at the time of first testing were further behind academically at first testing than those who were still in French immersion. The French immersion success group performed considerably in advance of grade level on the academic achievement test at the time of first testing.

The mean discrepancy scores for first testing and retesting for the actual grade level and expected grade level for the three French immersion difficulty sub-groups and the French immersion success group are presented in Table XXXIII.

Insert Table XXXIII About Here

The English-English group was furthest behind expected grade level at first testing and again at second testing. However, this group appeared to be making the most improvement at the time of second testing with regard to actual grade level compared to the other two difficulty groups, that is, the French immersion-French immersion group and French immersion-English group. At first testing, the three French immersion difficulty groups were doing best in arithmetic, however, by the time of second testing, these groups had a change in score ratio somewhat and were the least behind in reading. The French immersion success group was the most advanced in reading and spelling at both testings. In terms of expected grade level, all groups were behind a little more at second testing in all areas with the exception of the French immersion-French immersion group and the English-English group which had attained their same relative position in reading on both testings. In terms of actual grade level, the French immersion-French immersion group and the French immersion-English group improved in reading only, while the English-English group

TABLE XXXIII

Mean WRAT Discrepancy Scores[1] at First and Second Testing for Actual and Expected Grade Levels for the Four Comparison Groups

First Testing	French Immersion-French Immersion	French Immersion-English	English-English	French Immersion Success
Reading:				
Actual	.45	.57	.6	-1.26
Expected	.4	.57	1.1	-1.4
Spelling:				
Actual	.52	.39	1.63	-.81
Expected	.77	.53	1.3	-.96
Arithmetic:				
Actual	.01	.13	.02	-.09
Expected	.25	.41	.52	-.51

Second Testing				
Reading:				
Actual	.23	.23	-.1	-.8
Expected	.48	.66	1.1	-.94
Spelling:				
Actual	.87	.57	.47	-.74
Expected	1.12	1.0	1.63	-.89
Arithmetic:				
Actual	.35	.36	-0.7	.14
Expected	.59	.79	1.15	-.27

[1] A positive discrepancy score indicates that the achievement score was below actual or expected grade level. A negative score indicates that the achievement score was above actual or expected grade level.

improved in all areas tested. The French immersion success group, although above grade level except in arithmetic at second testing, lost some ground in all areas.

ii) Discrepancy Scores Frequencies

The frequency of subjects at the time of first testing in the French immersion difficulty group (N=32) scoring below actual grade level as compared to at or above grade level are as follows:

	Actual Gr. Level				Expected Gr. Level			
	Below		At/Above		Below		At/Above	
	Frequency	%	Frequency	%	Frequency	%	Frequency	%
Reading	22	68.8	9	28.1	24	75	8	25
Spelling	26	81.2	6	18.8	26	81.2	6	18.8
Arithmetic	15	46.9	17	53.1	20	62.5	12	37.5

The complete breakdown for all sub-groups at the time of first and second testing is presented in Appendix 9.

Several trends emerged through inspecting the frequency data. There was a tendency for the groups of subjects who switched to English language programs to have a higher percentage of subjects performing below actual or expected grade levels in reading on first testing as compared to subjects who remained in French immersion. On retesting, these groups showed some improvement but a higher percentage was still below grade level as compared to subjects who remain in French immersion. In all difficulty groups there was a high percentage of subjects doing poorly in spelling at both testings. With regards to arithmetic, in all difficulty groups there was a high percentage of subjects doing poorly (in no case did a percentage as high as 45% of the group perform at or above expected levels in arithmetic) and there was a tendency for all groups by the time of second testing to show higher rates of difficulty in arithmetic and it was most evident in the groups which switched to English programming. For the French immersion success group there were very high percentages of subjects scoring at or above expected grade levels at first testing. Although this group continues to have the highest percentage of subjects scoring at or above expected grade level at second testing, there was a decrease from their advantage at first testing.

    iii) Discrepancy Scores: Difference Scores Between First and Second Testing:

Difference scores were calculated for the two types of discrepancy scores by subtracting the discrepancy score at second testing from that at first testing. A negative difference score indicates better performance at first testing, i.e. decrease in the level of functioning, while a positive difference score indicates better performance at second testing, i.e. improved functioning. Individual difference scores based on actual grade level discrepancy scores and expected grade level discrepancy scores are included in Appendix 10. The mean difference scores for the four comparison groups are presented in Table XXXIV. It can be seen from

---

Insert Table XXXIV About Here

Part A of Table XXXIV that the French immersion-English and the English-English groups improved more in terms of actual grade level discrepancy scores from first to second testing than did the French immersion-French immersion group. Based on individual data presented in Appendix 10, it can be seen that the 13 children in the English language programming, 54% improved in reading versus 43% in the French immersion-French

TABLE XXXIV

Mean Difference Scores[1] for Actual and Expected Grade Level WRAT Discrepancy Scores for the Four Comparison Groups

	French Immersion-French Immersion	French Immersion-English	English-English	French Immersion Success
Actual Grade Level (A)				
Reading	-.2	.2	.7	-.46
Spelling	.25	-.07	.35	-.07
Arithmetic	-.35	-.16	.08	-.56
Expected Grade Level (B)				
Reading	-.24	-.17	.03	-.41
Spelling	-.39	-.26	-.33	-.07
Arithmetic	-.33	-.19	-.63	-.34

[1] A positive difference score indicates better performance at follow-up testing. A negative difference score indicates better performance at first testing.

immersion group: 46% in spelling versus 20% in the French immersion-French immersion group and 46% in arithmetic versus 20% in the French immersion-French immersion group. Of the two groups who had switched to English, the English-English group showed the greatest improvement and their improvement was evident in all areas versus an improvement in reading only in the French immersion-English group. This improvement may be a function of the duration of time in the English language program. These findings are of great importance since they are at variance with the prediction in the Bruck, Rabinovitch and Oates (1975) study. Although the authors did not have adequate follow-up information, they speculated that it is advisable to leave a child in French immersion even though he is having difficulty since he would experience the same difficulty in an English language program. There is strong evidence from these follow-up scores that this is not the case. The French immersion success group, as a whole, was less in advance of actual grade levels at the time of second testing than at first. These children tended to maintain their relative advantage at the time of second testing in spelling only. As can be seen from the difference scores based on expected grade level discrepancy, Part B of Table XXXIV, a number of the same trends are maintained. It is interesting with the English-English group in particular, that there was a slight improvement in reading levels over the test-retest interval. Aside for this, and on the whole, the French immersion difficulty groups performed more poorly on second testing than on first. The French immersion success group also performed somewhat more poorly on second testing.

iv) Test de Rendement en Français Results

The level of the Rendement en Français (1973-74) was selected according to actual grade placement for each child still in a French immersion program. For children who had switched to English, the level of the Rendement en Français was selected according to the grade placement in French immersion prior to the switch to an English language program. The mean stanine score for the French immersion difficulty group was 1.88 and for the French immersion success group was 3.0. Subdividing the French immersion group into three separate groups, the mean stanine scores were as follows: French immersion-French immersion difficulty group 2.3, French immersion-English group 1.5 and English-English group 1.6. The mean score for the two groups who had switched to English was 1.44. In general, it is clear from inspection of individual trends that those children who do well on the Rendement are the same children who are good readers on the English academic achievement test.

DISCUSSION

It was pointed out in the Introduction to this study, that the early French immersion programs in Montreal, Ottawa and Toronto are noteworthy for their reported successes. However, the studies can generally be criticized for failing to specify attrition rates and, more importantly, to identify the reasons for children dropping out of the French immersion program. It is just as important to define the characteristics of the marginally successful student and the failing student as it is to outline the factors involved in regards to the students who are successfully maintained in the program. Many variables appear to be involved in successful and unsuccessful progress in a second language program.

The urgent need for a detailed investigation into the reasons for failure in a French immersion program evolved out of the fact that by 1973, increasing numbers of referrals of children from French immersion programs were being made to the Neuropsychology Laboratory of the Royal Ottawa Hospital. It was apparent that, after intensive investigation, these children could not be readily classified as having a more standard type of difficulty such as congenital-familial dyslexia, minimal brain dysfunction, hyperactivity or primary emotional disturbance. It was considered possible, that if these children were in an English language program, their progress through school might have been uneventful. A survey of the literature indicated that there were no guidelines for identifying high risk children. In an attempt to identify the characteristics of the children who have difficulty in a French immersion program, a group of 32 subjects was composed and compared with seven control groups matched as closely as possible for age and sex. The French immersion group, however, was younger, had higher IQ scores than most of the other groups, and had a higher percentage of females and left handers. The results of the present study substantiate the view that children who experience difficulty in French immersion are unique in terms of the factors contributing to their learning disability. An examination of the diagnostic labels originally assigned to these children, indicated that they could not be readily classified into any of the standard learning disability groups and, thus, other factors appeared to be involved.

Using a discriminant function analysis, it was remarkable that a statistically significant number of subjects were correctly classified into the eight comparison groups. This high rate of correct classification in a complex eight group analysis is very unusual in the behavioural sciences. The fact that the French immersion subjects were significantly differentiated from other groups experiencing difficulty in school, supported the hypothesis that this group is unique, as are the other groups, in terms of an individual test profile. This supports the notion that unique factors are operating in the learning difficulties of the French immersion group and they cannot as a group be considered to have more "classical" origins of the learning problems such as dyslexia, hyperactivity, minimal brain dysfunction or personality and behaviour problems.

Characteristics of Children who have Difficulty in French Immersion

The three language control groups had lower verbal intelligence than the four problem groups and the French immersion group. On the basis of IQ tests alone, the problems seem to be quite different in the French immersion group as compared to the three language control groups in that low intelligence may well be implicated in the language groups with learning difficulty, but the French immersion group stood out for its high IQ. In spite of the above average intelligence it was quite striking to find that the French immersion subjects stayed below the 50th percentile on the Wide Range Achievement Test for reading as they got older. The French immersion group performed relatively well, as compared to the learning disability groups on tests of reading and spelling, however, at all times their performance, when compared to a normal reference group, was far below average which seemed even more noticeable when it was recalled that their IQ's were well above average.

It was most interesting to note the results on the Illinois Test of Psycholinguistic Ability in that there were no significant differences among the groups. Therefore, the French immersion experience did not enhance psycholinguistic abilities as measured by this test, nor were poor psycholinguistic abilities associated with poor progress in the second language program. This finding is somewhat at variance with the Edwards and Casserley (1971, 1972, 1973) results and will be monitored carefully in further follow-up studies. On a measure of speech-sound discrimination (Boston Speech Sound Discrimination Test) there was no evidence that familiarity with more than one language facilitated speech-sound discrimination and, in fact, all groups did fairly poorly on this test (lowest quartile). This finding will also be looked at very carefully in a follow-up study in which good and poor performers in a French immersion program will be compared.

It was clear on the basis of the eight group analysis that no single factor or test measure differentiated the French immersion group from all other groups. Although the subjects could be reliably assigned to their groups and there were clear group differences, the differentiation could not be determined on the basis of a single test or factor. Intelligence tests were the best differentiators between the French immersion group and the three language control groups with the French immersion group, as stated earlier, having the highest IQ scores. However, a potentially very significant trend did emerge in that the French immersion group obtained poorer scores on the Tactual Performance Test (TPTOTT) which is a complex psychomotor problem-solving task administered under blindfold conditions. This finding was quite striking in that the French immersion group, although more intelligent, with superior motor and sensory functions, had at the same time, substantial difficulty on this psychomotor problem-solving measure. This deficit could be interpreted as secondary to a maturational deficit in the temporal lobe region. It is well established that auditory perceptual and associated memory functions are subserved by temporal lobe structures. One could speculate that since the primary auditory cortex is situated in the temporal lobes, children who have a mild maturational deficit affecting these areas would have difficulty in a complex language learning situation. The proposition that certain language learning deficits are related to maturational deficits in specific brain areas is not new. Recently, some writers have been postulating a specific maturational deficit in posterior brain regions in dyslexics (Satz and Sparrow, 1970), however one does not necessarily have to view these deficits within a developmental framework (Trites and Fiedorowicz, in press).

In the two group discriminant function analysis, it was once again clear that a very high percentage of correct classifications were made. In terms of specific test scores, there was evidence of a low reading achievement level for the anglophones in francophone schools, francophones in francophone schools and the reading disability children. The performance intelligence factor (PRFINTOT) was important in differentiating the French immersion group from all but the reading disability group, while the WISC Verbal IQ and the Peabody IQ of the verbal intelligence factor (VRBINTOT) were important in differentiating the French immersion from the ethnic groups in anglophone schools and francophones in francophone schools. This low verbal ability may be an important consideration of the learning problem of these two language groups, but not with the French immersion group.

Considering the discrepancy between the Verbal IQ and Performance IQ, the Performance IQ was higher than the Verbal IQ for all groups. The group that had the smallest discrepancy was the French immersion success group, which was also the only group in the study selected for doing well in school.

Follow-up Testing

The majority of the children in the French immersion difficulty group and in the French immersion success group were brought in for follow-up testing on a variety of measures. Several questions were of concern here, including the academic status of children who had been enrolled in French immersion but were switched to an English language program. Additional valuable data was gathered on the subsequent outcome of children who have difficulty in French immersion but are maintained in that program, and the continued progress of a small group of children in French immersion who were successfully completing the program. The characteristics of children who have difficulty in French immersion programs were also focused upon in the follow-up assessment.

a) Behavioural and Personality Data

As might be expected, children who have had difficulty in French immersion, irrespective of whether or not they are still in the program, generally obtained higher profile scores (i.e. more of a problem) on the Connors Teacher's Questionnaire rating scales, particularly on the inattentive-passivity scale and the hyperactivity scale. It is quite possible, that the child presenting with a combination of difficulty in French immersion, plus being hyperactive, has a very high profile for the teacher. Conceivably the passive, more hypoactive child may have the same degree of difficulty in French immersion but may not be detected. Personality test data on some of the children indicated that they can be characterized as impulsive, enthusiastic, activity-oriented and sociable. Occasionally these children have difficulty functioning effectively and maintaining their motivation in a highly structured, controlled and more traditionally oriented program.

b) Questionnaire Responses

The children's responses to a questionnaire at the follow-up assessment indicated that those who had difficulty in French immersion did not, on the whole, differ in attitudes from children who were successful in this program. However, children who remained in French immersion, although having difficulty, tended to have a more positive attitude towards the program than those who switched to an English language program.

When family background was considered, there was a higher incidence of reading difficulty in the families of the French immersion difficulty group as compared to the group of children who were successful in the program. In addition, parents of the children having difficulty tended to view their child's problem as a reading difficulty. They worried about their child's progress in learning the regular school subjects through the medium of French. There was a higher incidence of busing the children to school in the French immersion difficulty group. The busing may have been a burden in both academic progress and social relationships.

In general, all parents wanted their children to learn to speak French. However, more parents of the children who were successful in French immersion had themselves attempted to learn to speak French and expressed positive attitudes towards learning French themselves as compared to parents of the difficulty group. Success group parents thus tended to express a stronger integrative orientation towards learning to speak French than did the difficulty group parents. These strong positive attitudes of the success group parents may have strengthened positive attitudes in their children and contributed, to some extent, to the child's success in French immersion. This can be interpreted in the light of Gardner and Lambert's (1959) findings that an integrative orientation facilitates second language learning. It should be noted, however, that the responses of the children themselves failed to reveal differences in attitude between the successful and unsuccessful groups.

Background information questions also revealed some differences between the groups of children who remained in French immersion although they were having difficulty and those who switched to an English language program. Parental attitudes seemed to be responsible for a child continuing in the French immersion program although having difficulty. More of the parents who maintained their children in French immersion would enroll another child in a French immersion program, were less worried about their child's success in learning regular subjects through French, about his reading ability and about his relationship with the French immersion teacher, as compared to parents who switched their children to an English language program. In addition, these parents had a more integrative orientation towards second language learning compared to the parents of switches to English. More parents of switches considered that that their children disliked French immersion and were shy, withdrawn and a behaviour problem in that program.

c) Test Scores of the French Immersion Difficulty Groups and the French Immersion Success Group

A comparison of the various test scores between the French immersion difficulty group and the French immersion success group indicated that the success group had higher Verbal IQ's, higher academic achievement scores, higher performance scores on auditory and visual memory tests and better behaviour adjustment ratings.

An important finding was that there was some evidence that children who have difficulty in French immersion but who are retained in that program, suffer in comparison to children who have been switched to an English language program. This was seen as a noticeable improvement in vocabulary scores among the children who were switched to an English language program, tendency toward improvement in reading vocabulary and greater relative improvement on Wide Range Achievement Test scores. The children who were switched to English programming improved more in terms of actual grade level discrepancy scores from first to second testing than did the children who were having difficulty in French immersion but maintained in that program. The French immersion success group was less in advance of actual grade level at follow-up testing than they were at first testing. These preliminary findings are extremely important and they are at variance with the prediction of Bruck, <u>et al</u> (1975). They speculated that it is advisable to leave a child in French immersion even though he is having difficulty since he would experience the same difficulty in an English language program. There is a strong indication from the present follow-up study that this is not the case.

Bruck, <u>et al</u> (1975) also suggested that the child in French immersion experiences a difficult period from the end of grade one through some of grade two but that schoolwork then becomes easier. In addition, several of the follow-up studies of children in French immersion have concluded that the child may experience difficulty in grade one and through some of grade two, but then they quickly make up for their deficiencies, for example, in English language reading. However, it must be emphasized that these conclusions are based upon the test scores of those select children who have remained in the French immersion programs. Consideration of the follow-up test results on a small group of French immersion difficulty children who remained in French immersion, indicate that for this group of children, there was not an improvement after grade two and, in fact, some children who had an early acceleration in reading and spelling lost this advantage by the end of grade two. This point is merely made to emphasize that there are substantial individual differences in rates of progress.

With regard to the effect of French immersion programming upon reading skills, little can be said. Children who switched to an English language program did make greater relative gains in reading ability from first to second testing which suggests that reading in the vernacular had beneficial effects. In addition, the French immersion success group was less in advance of actual grade level at second testing compared to first testing indicating some slowing in the rate of progress. However, these results are not necessarily at variance with results reported by others which indicate that French immersion programming is not detrimental to academic progress, since a different measure of progress was employed in the present study. Instead of rating the child as at or below grade level, the use of discrepancy scores between academic achievement scores and actual and expected grade levels allows one to examine the relative acceleration of academic levels at various grade levels. It is suggested that further follow-up studies consider discrepancy scores and relative rates of acceleration.

Certainly it is clear that the results of this study point strongly toward a specific syndrome or sub-skill deficits in children who fail in early French immersion programs. There are obviously many different reasons to consider in this study regarding school failure. With respect to etiology of language learning disorders in general, a great deal must be learned. For example, an international authority on language disorders, Dr. Isabella Rapin of the U.S.A., has just reported a very high frequency of more than one language in the homes (57 out of 100 subjects) of a group of children with language impairment versus only 12 out of 100 in a hearing impaired group (Rapin, 1975).

The results of this study have a bearing on several aspects of French immersion programming. For example, a child who is hyperactive should not be screened out on the basis of the hyperactivity. In fact none of the other standard diagnostic categories such as dyslexia, minimal cerebral dysfunction or behaviour adjustment problems characterize the French immersion difficulty group. This latter group presents a unique profile of deficits. If a child is in a French immersion course but clearly not progressing satisfactorily, careful consideration should be given to a switch to an English language program. There is no evidence to suggest that the student will catch up if he remains in French immersion, or that he will have equal difficulty in the English program.

Proposed Study for 1975-1976

The focus of this project for the next year will be on the following four points:

1. Repeat follow-up of the children so far extensively studied.
2. Comparison will be made between 20 children who have dropped out

of a French immersion program matched with their classmates who are still in French immersion and who started in the same French immersion class and had the same teachers.

    3. The intensive studies of the matched-pair groups will include an extensive battery of reading sub-skill tests devised by Dr. Donald Doehring, Research Director, School of Human Communication Disorders at McGill University. The focus of this study will be to see if there are particular reading sub-skill patterns characteristic of the French immersion difficulty group.

    4. By cross-validating the findings of the first study and possibly extending the findings based on the results of the second year study, an attempt will be made to identify those factors which should be considered in developing a screening assessment. At the present time, there does not appear to be any formal screening criteria. Students who do not succeed in French immersion tend to repeat one or more grades and this has its obvious attendant problems.

BIBLIOGRAPHY

Alexander, D., Hallows, S. and Tiltens, M., An Investigation of Factors which may have Contributed to Children Dropping Out of French Immersion at Rosyln School, unpublished paper completed under the direction of R.C. Tucker for Rosyln School Committee and Sir George Williams University, Montreal, 1974.

Barik, H.C. and Swain, M., Bilingual Education Project: Evaluation of the 1972-73 French Immersion Kindergarten and Grade One Classes at Allenby Public School in Toronto, Toronto: Ontario Institute for Studies in Education, 1973.

--------, Bilingual Education Project: Evaluation of the 1973-74 French Immersion Program in Grades 1-3 in the Federal Capital's Public Schools. Toronto: Ontario Institute for Studies in Education, 1974a.

--------, Bilingual Education Project: Evaluation of the 1971-72 and 1972-73 French Immersion Program in Grades 8 and 9, Peel County Board of Education. Unpublished research report, Toronto: Ontario Institute of Studies, 1974b.

--------, "Three-Year Evaluation of a Large Scale Early French Immersion Program: The Ottawa Study," Language Learning, Vol. 25, 1975, p. 1-30.

Barik, H.C., Swain, M. and McTavish, K., Bilingual Education Project: Evaluation of the 1973-74 French Immersion Program in Grades K-2 at Allenby Public School, Toronto, Toronto: Ontario Institute for Studies in Education, 1974.

Barkman, L.B., "Some Psychological Perspectives on Bilingualism and Second Language Teaching," McGill Journal of Education, Vol. 4, 1969, p. 45-58.

Bruck, M., Lambert, W.E. and Tucker, G.R., Cognitive and Attitudinal Consequences of Bilingual Schooling: The St. Lambert Project Through Grade Six. Unpublished Research Report, Montreal: McGill University, 1973.

--------, "Bilingual Schooling Through the Elementary Grades: The St. Lambert Project at Grade Seven," Language Learning, Vol. 24, 1974, p. 183-203.

--------, Assessing Functional Bilingualism Within a Bilingual Program: The St. Lambert Project at Grade Eight. Unpublished Research Report, Montreal: McGill University, Undated.

Bruck, M., Rabinovitch, M.S. and Oates, M., "The Effects of French Immersion Programs on Children with Language Disabilities - A preliminary report," Working Papers on Bilingualism, Issue No. 5. Toronto: Ontario Institute for Studies in Education, 1975.

Carroll, J.B., Psychological and Educational Research into Second Language Teaching to Young Children. In H.H. Stern (Ed.), Languages and the Young School Child. London: Oxford University Press, 1969, p. 56-68.

Dockrell, W.B. and Brosseau, J.F., "The Correlates of Second Language Learning by Young Children," Alberta Journal of Educational Research, vol. 13, 1967, p. 295-298.

Downing, John, Bilingualism and Learning to Read: A Cross-Cultural Approach. Unpublished Paper, Victoria: University of Victoria, Undated.

Edwards, H.P. and Casserly, M.C. Research and Evaluation of the French Program 1970-71 annual report, Ottawa: The Ottawa Roman Catholic School Board, 1971.

--------. Research and evaluation of second language programs: 1971-72 annual report, Ottawa: The Ottawa Roman Catholic Separate School Board, 1972.

--------, Evaluation of Second Language Programs in the English Schools. Annual Report, 1972-73. Ottawa: The Ottawa Roman Catholic Separate School Board, 1973.

Gardner, R.C., Motivational Variables in Second Language Learning. Research Bulletin #298, London: University of Ontario, 1974.

Gardner, R.C. and Lambert, W.E., "Motivational Variables in Second Language Acquisition," Canadian Journal of Psychology, vol. 13, 1959, p. 266-272.

Gardner, R.C. and Smythe, P.C., The Integrative Motive in Second Language Acquisition. Research Bulletin #275, London: University of Western Ontario, 1973.

Gezi, Kal, "Bilingual-Bicultural Education: A Review of Relevant Research," California Journal of Educational Research, vol. 25, 1974, p. 223-239.

Jones, W.R., Bilingualism in Welsh Education. Cardiff: University of Wales Press, 1966.

Kirk, Roger E., Experimental Design: Procedures for the Behavioural Sciences. Balmont, California: Brooks/Cole Publishing Company, 1968.

Lambert, W.E., Tucker, G.R. and D'Anglejan, A., "Cognitive and Attitudinal Consequences of Bilingual Schooling: The St. Lambert Project Through Grade Five," Journal of Educational Psychology, vol. 65, 1973, p. 141-159.

Lambert, W.E. and Tucker, G.R., Bilingual Education of Children: The St. Lambert Experiment. Rowley, Massachusetts: Newbury House, 1972.

Mackey, W.F., The Lesson to be Learned from Bilingualism. In P.R. Leon (Ed.), *Applied Linguistics and the Teaching of French.* Montreal: Centre Educatif et Culturel, 1967, p. 53-62.

Macnamara, John, *Bilingualism in Primary Education: A Study of Irish Experience.* Edinburgh: University Press, 1966.

Miller, George A. (Ed.), *Linguistic Communication: Perspectives for Research.* Newark, Delaware: International Reading Association, 1973.

Modiano, N., "National or mother language in beginning reading: a comparative study," *Research in the Teaching of English,* vol. 2, 1968, p. 32-43.

Nie, N., Hull, C.H., Jenkins, J., Steinbrenner, K., and Bent, D.H., *Statistical Package for the Social Sciences (SPSS),* Second Edition. McGraw-Hill, 1975.

Paulston, C.B., "Ethnic Relations and Bilingual Education: Accounting for Contradictory Data," *Working Papers on Bilingualism,* Issue No. 6, Toronto: Ontario Institute for Studies in Education, 1975.

Penfield, Wilder, "Conditioning of the Uncommitted Cortex for Language Learning," *Brain,* vol. 88, 1965, p. 787-798.

Pimsleur, P., Stockwell, R.P. and Comrey, A.L., "Foreign Language Learning Ability," *Journal of Educational Psychology,* vol. 53, 1962, p. 15-26.

Rapin, I., *Children with Language Disability.* Paper presented at the First International Congress of Child Neurology. Toronto, 1975.

Satz, P. and Sparrow, S. Specific developmental dyslexia: a theoretical formulation. In D. Bakker and P. Satz (Eds.), *Specific Reading Disability: Advances in Theory and Method.* Rotterdam: Universitaire Pers Rotterdam, 1970.

Stern, H.H., *Foreign Languages in Primary Education.* London: Oxford University Press, 1967.

Swain, M., *Early and Late French Immersion Programs in Canada: Research Findings.* Paper presented at the Federal-Provincial Conference on Bilingualism in Education, Halifax, Nova Scotia, 1974.

Trites, R. and Fiedorowicz, C. Follow-up Study of Children with Specific (or Primary) Reading Disability. In D. Bakker and R. Knights (Eds.), *The Neuropsychology of Learning Disorders: Theoretical Approaches.* Baltimore: University Park Press, in press, January, 1976.

Tucker, G.R., The Development of Reading Skills Within a Bilingual Education Program. Unpublished paper. McGill University, Montreal, 1974.

Tucker, G.R., Lambert, W.E. and D'Anglejan, A., Are French Immersion Programs Suitable for Working Class Children? A Pilot Investigation. Unpublished Research Report, McGill University, Montreal, 1972.

UNESCO: Report of an International Seminar on Bilingualism in Education, Aberstwyth, Wales. London: Her Majesty's Stationary Office, 1965.

APPENDIX 1

FRENCH IMMERSION PROGRAMS IN THE NATIONAL CAPITAL AREA

Four school boards in this area offer early French immersion programming. In the Ottawa and Carleton Public School boards French immersion kindergarten was introduced in September of 1970. In kindergarten and grade one all instruction is in French, including reading and writing. English language arts are introduced for one hour daily in grade two with the amount of English instruction increasing with each advancing grade. A few schools delay the teaching of English reading until grade three, which is the pattern followed in the Ottawa Roman Catholic Separate Schools. Beginning in 1969, this board offered a bilingual kindergarten program in which instruction was in English for half the day and in French for the remaining half. In grades one and two all instruction is in French, with the exception of religious education, and English language skills are introduced in grade three.

The Carleton Roman Catholic Separate School Board follows the same procedure as the other Separate School Board with the exception that in grade three English and French are each used as the language of instruction for 50% of the curriculum.

APPENDIX 2

QUESTIONNAIRES: FAMILY HISTORY OF READING PROBLEMS, CONNORS PARENT'S
QUESTIONNAIRE, CONNORS TEACHER'S QUESTIONNAIRE, THE PUPIL RATING SCALE

FAMILY HISTORY OF READING PROBLEMS

I. **Parents**

   A. Mother:
      1. Do you have any reading difficulty?
         Yes _____ No _____
      2. Do you read a daily newspaper?
         Yes _____ No _____ If so, which newspaper?
         _____
      3. Do you read any magazines?
         Yes _____ No _____ If so, what magazines?
         _____
      4. Do you read books?
         Yes _____ No _____ If so, what books have you read recently? _____
      5. What is the highest grade you completed in school? _____
      6. Occupation _____

   B. Father:
      1. Do you have any reading difficulty?
         Yes _____ No _____
      2. Do you read a daily newspaper?
         Yes _____ No _____ If so, which newspaper?
      3. Do you read magazines?
         Yes _____ No _____ If so, what magazines?
      4. Do you read books?
         Yes _____ No _____ If so, what books have you read recently? _____
      5. What is the highest grade you completed in school? _____
      6. Occupation _____

II. **Siblings**

   A. Do you have any other children?
      Yes _____ No _____
   B. Have any of them had difficulty in learning how to read?
      Yes _____ No _____ Any present reading problems?
      Yes _____ No _____
   C. Have any of your children ever been held back a year in school?
      Yes _____ No _____
   D. What is the highest grade that each of your children have completed in school?
      ___ ; ___ ; ___ ; ___ ; ___ ; ___ ; ___ ;

III. **Mother's siblings**

   A. Have any of your brothers or sisters had any reading difficulty? Yes _____ No _____
   B. What was the highest grade completed in school by each of them? ___ ; ___ ; ___ ; ___ ; ___ ; ___ ; .

IV. **Father's siblings**

   A. Have any of your brothers or sisters had any reading difficulty? Yes _____ No _____
   B. What was the highest grade completed in school by each of them? ___ ; ___ ; ___ ; ___ ; ___ ; ___ ; .

V. **Grandparents**

   A. Mother's parents:
      1. Has either your mother or father had any reading difficulty? Yes _____ No _____
         If so, which one? _____
      2. What grade did your mother complete? _____
         father? _____
   B. Father's parents:
      1. Has either your mother your father had any reading difficulty? Yes _____ No _____
         If so, which one? _____
      2. What grade did your mother complete? _____
         father? _____

VI. **Other relatives**

   A. Mother's relatives:
      1. Have any other relatives in your family had reading difficulties? Yes _____ No _____
         If so, which one? _____
         Grade level _____
   B. Father's relatives
      1. Have any other relatives in your family had reading difficulties? Yes _____ No _____
         If so, which one? _____
         Grade level _____

VII. **Subject**

   A. Did subject have any difficulty learning to read? _____
   B. Was subject ever held back in school because of the difficulty? _____
   C. Does the subject do much reading outside of school work? _____
   D. Does the subject read:
      1. A daily newspaper? _____
      2. Any magazines? _____
      3. Any books? _____
      4. Comic books? _____

III. **Comments** _____
_____
_____
_____
_____

TRITES, OTTA

CONNORS PARENT'S QUESTIONNAIRE

Name of Child _____   Date _____

Your Name _____   Relationship _____

Instructions: Listed below are items concerning children's behaviour or the problems they sometimes have. Read each item carefully and decide how much you think your child has been bothered by this problem *during the past month* —
NOT AT ALL, JUST A LITTLE, PRETTY MUCH or VERY MUCH

Indicate your choice by placing a check mark (√) in the appropriate column to the right of each item.

ANSWER ALL ITEMS

Observation	Not at All	Just a little	Pretty Much	Very much
PROBLEMS OF EATING				
1. Picky and finicky				
2. Will not eat enough				
3. Overweight				
PROBLEMS OF SLEEP				
4. Restless				
5. Nightmares				
6. Awakens at night				
7. Cannot fall asleep				
FEAR AND WORRIES				
8. Afraid of new situations				
9. Afraid of people				
10. Afraid of being alone				
11. Worries about illness and death				
MUSCULAR TENSION				
12. Gets stiff and rigid				
13. Twitches, jerks, etc.				
14. Shakes				
SPEECH PROBLEMS				
15. Stuttering				
16. Hard to understand				
WETTING				
17. Bed wetting				
18. Runs to bathroom constantly				
BOWEL PROBLEMS				
19. Soiling self				
20. Holds back bowel movements				
COMPLAINS OF FOLLOWING SYMPTOMS EVEN THOUGH DOCTOR CAN FIND NOTHING WRONG				
21. Headaches				
22. Stomach aches				
23. Vomiting				
24. Aches and pains				
25. Loose bowels				
PROBLEMS OF SUCKING, CHEWING or PICKING				
26. Sucks thumb				
27. Bites or picks nails				
28. Chews on clothes, blankets, or others				
29. Picks at things such as hair, clothing, etc.				
CHILDISH OR IMMATURE				
30. Does not act his age				
31. Cries easily				
32. Wants help doing things he should do alone				
33. Clings to parents or other adults				
34. Baby talk				
TROUBLE WITH FEELINGS				
35. Keeps anger to himself				
36. Lets himself get pushed around by other children				
37. Unhappy				
38. Carries a chip on his shoulder				

TRITES, OTTAWA

ANSWER ALL ITEMS

Observation	Not at All	Just a little	Pretty much	Very much
OVER-ASSERTS HIMSELF				
39. Bullying				
40. Bragging and boasting				
41. Sassy to grown-ups				
PROBLEMS MAKING FRIENDS				
42. Shy				
43. Afraid they do not like him				
44. Feelings easily hurt				
45. Has no friends				
PROBLEMS WITH BROTHERS AND SISTERS				
46. Feels cheated				
47. Mean				
48. Fights constantly				
PROBLEMS KEEPING FRIENDS				
49. Disturbs other children				
50. Wants to run things				
51. Picks on other children				
RESTLESS				
52. Restless or over active				
53. Excitable, impulsive				
54. Fails to finish things he starts — short attention span				
TEMPER				
55. Temper outbursts, explosive and unpredictable behaviour				
56. Throws himself around				
57. Throws and breaks things				
58. Pouts and sulks				
SEX				
59. Plays with own sex organs				
60. Involved in sex play with others				
61. Modest about his body				
PROBLEMS IN SCHOOL				
62. Is not learning				
63. Does not like to go to school				
64. Is afraid to go to school				
65. Daydreams				
66. Truancy				
67. Will not obey school rules				
LYING				
68. Denies having done wrong				
69. Blames others for his mistakes				
70. Tells stories which did not happen				
STEALING				
71. From parents				
72. At school				
73. From stores and other places				
FIRE-SETTING				
74. Sets fires				
TROUBLE WITH POLICE				
75. Gets into trouble with the police				
Why?				
PERFECTIONISM				
76. Everything must be just so				
77. Things must be done same way every time				
78. Sets goals too high				
ADDITIONAL PROBLEMS				
79. Inattentive, easily distracted				
80. Constantly fidgeting				
81. Cannot be left alone				
82. Always climbing				
83. A very early riser				
84. Will run around between mouthfuls at meals				

TRITES, OTTAWA

85.	Demands must be met immediately – easily frustrated				
86.	Cannot stand too much excitement				
87.	Laces and zippers are always open				
88.	Cries often and easily				
89.	Unable to stop a repetitive activity				
90.	Acts as if driven by a motor				
91.	Mood changes quickly and drastically				
92.	Poorly aware of surroundings or time of day				
93.	Still cannot tie his shoelaces				

I. Please add any problems you have with your child _____

II. How serious a problem do you think your child has at this time?
    (　) No Problem　　(　) Minor Problem　　(　) Serious Problem

V. Indicate the items you are most concerned about or those you think are the most important problems your child has by placing a circle around the number (1-93) of those items.

How would you rate the child's behaviour compared to other children the same age?
much worse _____ worse _____ about the same _____ better _____ much better _____

Please fill in the following information about each member of the child's immediate family. (Please print clearly).

NAME	Relationship To Child	Age	Date of Birth	Occupation (Grade if a Student)	General Health	Height	Weight

What did the child eat for breakfast *this* morning? (Specify Type of Cereal)

What is his *usual* breakfast?

What is the usual breakfast of the other children?

What school is the child presently attending?

Teacher's Name:　　　　　　　　　　　　　　Principal's Name:

TRITES, OTTAWA

CONNORS TEACHER'S QUESTIONNAIRE

V. Listed below are descriptive terms of behaviour. Place a check mark in the column which best describes this child. ANSWER ALL ITEMS.

Observation	Not at all	Just a little	Pretty much	Very much
CLASSROOM BEHAVIOUR				
1. Constantly fidgeting				
2. Hums and makes other odd noises				
3. Demands must be met immediately-easily frustrated				
4. Coordination poor				
5. Restless or overactive				
6. Excitable, impulsive				
7. Inattentive, easily distracted				
8. Fails to finish things he starts-short attention span				
9. Overly sensitive				
10. Overly serious or sad				
11. Daydreams				
12. Sullen or sulky				
13. Cries often and easily				
14. Disturbs other children				
15. Quarrelsome				
16. Mood changes quickly and drastically				
17. Acts "smart"				
18. Destructive				
19. Steals				
20. Lies				
21. Temper outbursts, explosive and unpredictable behaviour				
GROUP PARTICIPATION				
22. Isolates himself from other children				
23. Appears to be unaccepted by group				
24. Appears to be easily led				
25. No sense of fair play				
26. Appears to lack leadership				
27. Does not get along with opposite sex				
28. Does not get along with same sex				
29. Teases other children or interferes with their activities				
ATTITUDE TOWARD AUTHORITY				
30. Submissive				
31. Defiant				
32. Impudent				
33. Shy				
34. Fearful				
35. Excessive demands for teacher's attention				
36. Stubborn				
37. Overly anxious to please				
38. Uncooperative				
39. Attendance problem				

How would you rate this child's behaviour compared to other children the same age?

much worse ☐   worse ☐   about the same ☐   better ☐   much better ☐

Signature _____ Title _____ Date Signed _____

TRITES, OT

THE PUPIL RATING SCALE
Screening for Learning Disabilities

HELMER R. MYKLEBUST, Ed.D.
Department of Special Education, Northern Illinois University

PUPIL'S NAME _____ SEX _____ DATE _____
                                                   Year Month Day

RESIDENCE _____ BORN _____
                                                    Year Month Day

PARENTS _____ AGE _____
                                                   Years Months Days

SCHOOL _____

TEACHER _____ GRADE _____

SUMMARY OF SCORES

AUDITORY COMPREHENSION _____

SPOKEN LANGUAGE   _____   VERBAL SCORE   _____

ORIENTATION   _____

MOTOR COORDINATION   _____

PERSONAL-SOCIAL BEHAVIOR _____   NONVERBAL SCORE   _____

                                     TOTAL SCALE SCORE   _____

© 1971 by Grune & Stratton, Inc.,
757 Third Avenue, New York, N. Y. 10017

TO THE TEACHER

Some children have deficits in learning which distinguish them from others in their class. The Pupil Rating Scale was developed so that these children can be effectively identified.

Your are to rate each child in five *behavioral areas,* all of which are related to success in learning: *Auditory Comprehension, Spoken Language, Orientation, Motor Coordination,* and *Personal-Social Behavior.* The ratings are made on a five-point scale. A rating of 3 is average, ratings of 1 or 2 are below average, and ratings of 4 or 5 are above average. A rating of 1 is the lowest and a rating of 5 is the highest that can be given. Indicate your rating by circling the number that represents your judgment of the child's level of function. When making your evaluation, rate only one area of behavior at a time and bear in mind that a child may be learning well in some respects but not in others.

The purpose of the Pupil Rating Scale is to identify those children who have learning disabilities. It should not be used as an indicator of inferior potential nor of lack of opportunity to learn. It is important, therefore, that your ratings be made only on the basis of the items listed on the Scale.

Other precautions are that you have extensive opportunity for observing the child and that you carefully study the Manual before you make your ratings.

Behavioral Characteristics

AUDITORY COMPREHENSION

	RATING
COMPREHENDING WORD MEANINGS	
Extremely immature level of understanding	1
Fails to grasp simple word meanings; misunderstands words at grade level	2
Good grasp of vocabulary for age and grade	3
Understands all grade-level vocabulary as well as higher-level word meanings	4
Superior understanding of vocabulary; understands many abstract words	5
FOLLOWING INSTRUCTIONS	
Unable to follow instructions; always confused	1
Usually follows simple instructions but often needs individual help	2
Follows instructions that are familiar and not complex	3
Remembers and follows extended instructions	4
Unusually skillful in remembering and following instructions	5
COMPREHENDING CLASS DISCUSSIONS	
Unable to follow and understand class discussions; always inattentive	1
Listens but rarely understands well; mind often wanders	2
Listens and follows discussions according to age and grade	3
Understands well; benefits from discussions	4
Becomes involved; shows unusual understanding of material	5
RETAINING INFORMATION	
Almost total lack of recall; poor memory	1
Retains simple ideas and procedures if repeated	2
Average retention of materials; adequate memory for age and grade	3
Remembers information from various sources; good immediate and delayed recall	4
Superior memory for details and content	5

SCORE _____

PERSONAL-SOCIAL BEHAVIOR

	RATING
COOPERATION	
Continually disrupts classroom; unable to inhibit responses	1
Frequently demands attention; often speaks out of turn	2
Waits his turn; average for age and grade	3
Above average; cooperates well	4
Excellent ability; cooperates without adult encouragement	5
ATTENTION	
Never attentive; very distractible	1
Rarely listens; attention frequently wanders	2
Attention adequate for age and grade	3
Above average in attention; almost always attends	4
Always attends to important aspects; long attention span	5
ORGANIZATION	
Highly disorganized; very slovenly	1
Often disorganized in manner of working; inexact, careless	2
Maintains average organization of work; careful	3
Above-average organization; organizes and completes work	4
Highly organized; completes assignments in meticulous manner	5
NEW SITUATIONS (parties, trips, changes in routine)	
Becomes extremely excitable, totally lacking in self-control	1
Often overreacts; finds new situations disturbing	2
Adapts adequately for age and grade	3
Adapts easily and quickly with self-confidence	4
Excellent adaptation; shows initiative and independence	5
SOCIAL ACCEPTANCE	
Avoided by others	1
Tolerated by others	2
Liked by others; average for age and grade	3
Well liked by others	4
Sought by others	5
RESPONSIBILITY	
Rejects responsibility; never initiates activities	1
Avoids responsibility; limited acceptance of role for age	2
Accepts responsibility; adequate for age and grade	3
Above average in responsibility; enjoys responsibility; initiates and volunteers	4
Seeks responsibility; almost always takes initiative with enthusiasm	5
COMPLETION OF ASSIGNMENTS	
Never finishes even with guidance	1
Seldom finishes even with guidance	2
Average performance; follows through on assignments	3
Above-average performance; completes assignments without urging	4
Always completes assignments without supervision	5
TACTFULNESS	
Always rude	1
Usually disregards feelings of others	2
Average tact; behavior occasionally inappropriate socially	3
Above average in tactfulness; behavior rarely inappropriate socially	4
Always tactful; behavior never socially inappropriate	5

SCORE

SPOKEN LANGUAGE

	RATING
VOCABULARY	
Always uses immature, poor vocabulary	1
Limited vocabulary, primarily simple nouns; few precise, descriptive words	2
Adequate vocabulary for age and grade	3
Above-average vocabulary; uses numerous precise, descriptive words	4
High-level vocabulary; always uses precise words; conveys abstractions	5
GRAMMAR	
Always uses incomplete sentences with grammatical errors	1
Frequently uses incomplete sentences; numerous grammatical errors	2
Uses correct grammar; few errors in use of prepositions, verb tense, pronouns	3
Above average oral language; rarely makes grammatical errors	4
Always speaks in grammatically correct sentences	5
WORD RECALL	
Unable to recall the exact word	1
Often gropes for words to express himself	2
Occasionally searches for correct word; recall adequate for age and grade	3
Above average; rarely hesitates on a word	4
Always speaks well; never hesitates or substitutes	5
STORYTELLING--RELATING EXPERIENCES	
Unable to tell a comprehensible story	1
Difficulty relating ideas in a logical sequence	2
Average; adequate for age and grade	3
Above average; uses logical sequence	4
Exceptional; relates ideas in a logical, meaningful manner	5
FORMULATING IDEAS	
Unable to relate isolated facts	1
Difficulty relating isolated facts; incomplete and scattered ideas	2
Usually relates facts meaningfully; relates facts adequately for age and grade	3
Above average; relates facts and ideas well	4
Outstanding; always relates facts appropriately	5

SCORE _____

ORIENTATION

	RATING
JUDGING TIME	
Lacks grasp of meaning of time; always late or confused	1
Fair time concept; tends to dawdle; often late	2
Average time judgment; adequate for age and grade	3
Prompt; late only with good reason	4
Skillful in handling schedules; plans and organizes well	5
SPATIAL ORIENTATION	
Always confused; unable to navigate around school, playground, or neighborhood	1
Frequently gets lost in relatively familiar surroundings	2
Can maneuver in familiar locations; average ability for age and grade	3
Above average; rarely lost or confused	4
Adapts to new situations and locations; never lost	5
JUDGING RELATIONSHIPS (big-little, far-close, heavy-light)	
Judgments always inadequate	1
Makes elementary judgments successfully	2
Average judgments for age and grade	3
Accurate but does not generalize to new situations	4
Unusually precise judgments; generalizes to new situations and experiences	5
KNOWING DIRECTIONS	
Highly confused; unable to distinguish right-left, north-south-east-west	1
Sometimes exhibits confusion	2
Average; uses right-left, north-south-east-west	3
Good sense of direction; seldom confused	4
Excellent sense of direction	5

SCORE _____

MOTOR COORDINATION

GENERAL COORDINATION (walking, running, hopping, climbing)	
Very poorly coordinated; clumsy	1
Below average; awkward	2
Average for age; graceful	3
Above average; does well in motor activities	4
Excels in coordination	5
BALANCE	
Very poor balance	1
Below-average ability; falls frequently	2
Average ability for age; adequate equilibrium	3
Above average ability in activities requiring balance	4
Excels in balance	5
MANUAL DEXTERITY	
Very poor in manual dexterity	1
Awkward; below average in dexterity	2
Adequate dexterity for age; manipulates well	3
Above-average dexterity	4
Excels; readily manipulates new equipment	5

SCORE _____

APPENDIX 3

SPECIAL QUESTIONNAIRES: BACKGROUND
INFORMATION AND QUESTIONS FOR SUBJECT

CODING

Parents
Card 40

BACKGROUND INFORMATION

Code 10 for N/A

___ ___ ___ ___ ___ (22-26)   1. Other languages in the home:
         1. None
         2. French
         3. Other

___ ___ ___ ___ ___ (27-31)   2. Do any family members, excluding S, speak French?
         1. Mother
         2. Father
         3. Both parents
         4. Sibs
         5. All
         6. None

___ ___ ___ ___ ___ (32-36)   3. Would the parents like to learn to speak French?
         1. Mother
         2. Father
         3. Both
         4. Neither

___ ___ ___ ___ ___ (37-41)   4. Have the parents taken a French course other than in elementary and/or high school?
         1. Mother
         2. Father
         3. Both
         4. Neither

___ ___ ___ ___ ___ (42-46)   5. Parents' attitude to the course taken.
         1. Both favourable
         2. Both unfavourable
         3. Ambivalent
         4. One favourable and one unfavourable
         5. N/A

___ ___ ___ ___ ___ (47-51)   6. Do the parents plan to take a French course?
         1. Mother
         2. Father
         3. Both
         4. Neither

___ ___ ___ ___ ___ (52-56)   7. Parents' attitude to the possibility of taking a French course.
         1. Both favourable
         2. Both unfavourable
         3. Ambivalent
         4. One favourable and one unfavourable

___ ___ ___ ___ ___ (57-61)   8. Do the parents want their children to learn to speak French?
         1. Yes
         2. No

_ _ _ _ _ (62-66) 9. Why is it important to learn to speak French?
1. Integrative reasons
2. Instrumental reasons
3. Both of the above

(10-12) Do the parents encourage subject to:

_ _ _ _ _ (67-71) 10. Have French-speaking friends?
1. Yes
2. No

_ _ _ _ _ (72-76) 11. Watch French television programs?
1. Yes
2. No

_ _ _ _ _ (7-11) 12. Speak French at home?
1. Yes
2. No

(12-16) 13. Reasons for enrolling S in French immersion:
1. Integrative
2. Instrumental
3. Both of the above
4. No other program available

(17-21) 14. When the parents enrolled S in French immersion were they worried about the possibility of failure in this program?
1. Yes
2. No

SIBLINGS

_ _ _ _ _ (22-26) 15. Number of children in school:
1-1
2-2
etc.
0 code as 9
(if no children in school code all quest. as 10 for N/A)

_ _ _ _ _ (27-31) 16. Are any in French immersion now, or have any been in it in the past?
1. Yes
2. No

_ _ _ _ _ (32-36) 17. How many take French in school? 1-1, 2-2, etc.

_ _ _ _ _ (37-41) 18. Do they like their French programmes?
1. All - yes
2. All - no
3. Some yes, some no

_ _ _ _ _ (42-46) 19. Would they like to be in French immersion?
1. All - yes
2. All - no
3. Some yes, some no

_ _ _ _ _ (47-51) 20. Progress in French?
1. All good
2. All poor
3. Some good, some poor

_ _ _ _ _ (52-56)   21. Do they want to learn to speak French?
                         1. All yes
                         2. All no
                         3. Some yes, some no

_ _ _ _ _ (57-61)   22. Do they attempt to speak French?
                         1. All yes
                         2. All no
                         3. Some yes, some no

_ _ _ _ _ (62-66)   23. Do they laugh at S's attempts to speak French?
                         1. All yes
                         2. All no
                         3. Some yes, some no

_ _ _ _ _ (67-71)   24. Do they envy his opportunity to speak French?
                         1. All yes
                         2. All no
                         3. Some yes, some no

COMMUNITY

_ _ _ _ _ (72-76)   25. Does S have French-speaking friends?
                         1. Yes
                         2. No

_ _ _ _ _ (7-11)   26. Are S's friends in French immersion?
                         1. Yes
                         2. No

_ _ _ _ _ (12-16)   27. Is/was the French immersion program in the neighbourhood school?
                         1. Yes
                         2. No

_ _ _ _ _ (17-21)   28. Did/would transfer from French immersion to an English programme upset S's social relationships?
                         1. Yes
                         2. No

_ _ _ _ _ (22-26)   29. Did/would transfer to English involve the following changes?
                         1. Change in classroom, same school
                         2. Change to neighbourhood school
                         3. Change to a school requiring bussing

_ _ _ _ _ (30-32)   Does S attempt to speak French to his friends who are:

_ _ _ _ _ (27-31)   30. In French Immersion?
                         1. Yes
                         2. No

_ _ _ _ _ (32-36)   31. No in French immersion and English speaking?
                         1. Yes
                         2. No

_ _ _ _ _ (37-41)   32. To French-speaking children?
                        1. Yes
                        2. No

SCHOOL INFORMATION

_ _ _ _ _ (42-46)   1. Transfer information at First testing
                        1. Still in French immersion
                        2. Switched to English

_ _ _ _ _ (47-51)   2. Transfer infromation at second testing

                        1. Still in French immersion
                        2. Switched to English

_ _ _ _ _ (52-56)   3. Length of time in French immersion
                        --code in months, based on 10-month
                          school year

_ _ _ _ _ (57-61)   4. Length of time in English since the transfer
                        --in months
                        --if still in Fr.Imm., code 999

_ _ _ _ _ (62-66)   5. Are/were you satisfied with S's progress in
                       learning French while in French immersion?
                        1. Yes
                        2. No

_ _ _ _ _ (67-71)   6. How well does S understand French?
                        1. Well
                        2. Not as well as his classmates
                        3. No idea

_ _ _ _ _ (72-76)   7. How well does S express himself in French?
                        1. Well
                        2. Not as well as classmates
                        3. No idea
                        4. Never does

CARD 43

_ _ _ _ _ (7-11)   8. Language of beginning reading instruction:
                        1. English
                        2. French

_ _ _ _ _ (12-16)   9. Has S learned to read and write in French?
                        1. Yes
                        2. No

_ _ _ _ _ (17-21)   10. If yes, how well?
                        1. Good
                        2. Satisfactory
                        3. Poor
                        4. No idea
                        5. N/A

_ _ _ _ _ (22-26)   11. Has S learned to read and write in English?
                        1. Yes
                        2. No

_ _ _ _ _ (27-31) 12. If yes, how well?
1. Good
2. Satisfactory
3. Poor
4. To idea
5. N/A

_ _ _ _ _ (32-36) 13. Did/does S get along well with his French immersion teacher?
1. Yes
2. No

_ _ _ _ _ (37-41) 14. Did/does S get along better with other teachers (eg. gym, music, English)?
1. Yes
2. No
3. N/A

_ _ _ _ _ (42-46) 15. Were you worried about your child's success in learning the regular school subject's through the medium of French?
1. Yes
2. No

_ _ _ _ _ (47-51) 16. Are/were you satisfied with S's progress in other subjects while in French immersion?
1. Yes
2. No

_ _ _ _ _ (52-56) 17. Have you considered removing S, or any of your children, from French immersion?
1. Yes
2. No

_ _ _ _ _ (57-61) 18. Have you removed another child from French immersion?
1. Yes
2. No

_ _ _ _ _ (62-66) 19. Do you regret having enrolled S in French immersion?
1. Yes
2. No

_ _ _ _ _ (67-71) 20. Would you enroll another child in French immersion?
1. Yes
2. No

_ _ _ _ _ (72-76) 21. S's attitude towards school in French immersion.
1. Likes/liked it
2. Dislikes/disliked it.

CARD 44

_ _ _ _ _ (7-11) 22. S's attitude towards school in English programme.
1. Likes it.
2. Dislikes it

_ _ _ _ _ (12-16) 23. S's behaviour in school in French immersion:
1. Enthusiastic, well-behaved, participating
2. Shy, withdrawn, little participation
3. Behaviour problem
4. No complaints

_ _ _ _ _ (17-21) 24. S's behaviour in the English programme, of class:
1. Enthusiastic, well-behaved, participating
2. Shy, withdrawn, little participation
3. Behaviour problem
4. No complaints

_ _ _ _ _ (22-26) 25. Have school authorities, or anyone else, suggested that S be transferred to the English programme?
1. Yes
2. No

_ _ _ _ _ (26-31) 26. Reasons for suggestion of transfer:
1. Learning difficulty
2. Behaviour problem (hyperactivity, etc)
3. Emotional problem
4. No other programme available

_ _ _ _ _ (32-36) 27. What was your reaction?
1. Agreement
2. Disagreement

_ _ _ _ _ (37-41) 28. What options were presented to you?
1. English programme only
2. Continue in French immersion if desired
3. English programme with extra help
4. French immersion with extra help

_ _ _ _ _ (42-46) 29. If S was switched to English, who made the decision?
1. Patents
2. School authorities
3. Parents in consultation with school authorities.

_ _ _ _ _ (47-51) 30. Reasons for the switch from French immersion to English programme:
1. Learning difficulty
2. Behaviour problems
3. Emotional problems
4. No other programme available

_ _ _ _ _ (52-56) 31. For children now in the English programme, are you satisfied with S's progress?
1. Yes
2. No
10. N/A

QUESTIONS FOR SUBJECT

1. How often do you watch French T.V. programmes?
    1. Not at all
    2. Occasionally (once or twice per week)
    3. Frequently (more than twice per week)

2. How well do you understand radio and T.V. programmes in French?
    1. Not at all, or a few words
    2. Can follow with some difficulty
    3. Good comprehension

3. When you talk with your classmates (who know French as well as you do), which languages do you use when you meet after school, or on the way home, or even in class when the teacher can't hear?
    1. English
    2. French
    3. Both

*3. When you were in French immersion, when you talked with your classmates (who knew French as well as you did), which languages did you use when you met after school, or on the way home, or even in class when the teacher could not hear?

4. Do you think any of your family members (your mother, father, sisters or brothers) would make fun of you if they heard you speaking French?
    1. Yes
    2. No

5. Do you think any of your friends would make fun of you if they heard you speaking French?
    1. Yes
    2. No

6. Have you met any French-speaking children in your neighbourhood?
    1. Yes
    2. No

7. If yes, which language do you speak together?
    1. English
    2. French
    3. Both

8. Have you any very good friends who are French-speaking?
    1. Yes
    2. No

9. Would you rather have English-speaking or French-speaking friends?
    1. English
    2. French
    3. No preference

10. Would you like to play with more French-speaking children if you had the chance?
    1. Yes
    2. No

11. Do you want to learn to speak French?
    1. Yes
    2. No

12. If yes, for what reasons?
    1. Instrumental (eg. job opportunities)
    2. Integrative (eg. for cummunicating with people)
    3. Both of the **above**
    4. Just "like it" or just to know it

13. Do you enjoy studying French the way you do in school?
    1. Yes
    2. No

*13. Did you enjoy studying French the way you did in French immersion?

14. Would you rather be in a class where the teacher speaks English?
    1. Yes
    2. No

*14. Do you wish that you were still in French immersion?

15. Do you want to continue learning French?
    1. Yes
    2. No

16. Did/do you like your French immersion teacher?
    1. Yes
    2. No

17. Did/do you like your other teachers better?
    1. Yes
    2. No

*Form of question for children who have switched to the English program.

APPENDIX 4

FACTOR LOADINGS OBTAINED FOR TESTS IN
EACH OF THE FOUR FACTOR ANALYSES

Factor Loadings for Tests of General Intelligence and Academic Achievement

Variable	Factor A PRFINTOT	Factor B ACADTOT	Factor C VRBINTOT
WISCVIQ	0.36052	0.23650	0.74959
WISCPIQ	0.85324	0.02589	0.24163
PEABBA	0.03197	-0.21932	-0.01226
PEABIQ	0.24892	0.06728	0.69735
VINELAND	0.27698	0.06095	0.25536
WRARSS	0.14496	0.69439	0.30124
WRASSS	0.31889	0.85143	-0.02899
WRAASS	0.27678	0.46340	0.35379
MATRST	0.57764	0.08514	0.20185
DEVDRAWT	0.49316	0.29075	0.13994
CATOTT	0.41706	0.05655	0.27399

Factor Loadings for Perceptual Tests

Variable	Factor A PERCTOTA	Factor B PERCTOTB
PERCQUOT	0.37624	0.55503
MCANSCAL	0.87853	0.10953
RLDISCT	-0.00333	0.12204
BOSTONT	0.55851	-0.00319
KNOXMEMQ	0.00649	0.46713

Factor Loadings for Certain Motor and Lateral Dominance Tests

Variable	Factor A STEADCT	Factor B VERGCT	Factor C MAZECT	Factor D LATDOMLM
LATDOMHL	-0.11218	0.02647	0.05733	0.83310
LATDOMEL	-0.05775	0.04835	-0.09404	0.38981
LATDOMFL	0.01025	-0.09478	-0.10622	0.51764
LATDOMAL	0.04763	-0.04448	-0.02036	0.32003
LATDOMNL	-0.08155	-0.00722	-0.09394	-0.31237
MAZEDCT	0.24469	0.08554	0.71479	-0.06543
MAZENCT	0.22351	0.21576	0.82952	-0.02446
VERGDCT	0.10461	0.82657	0.13990	-0.04426
VERGNCT	0.02777	0.84759	0.11468	-0.02320
STEADDCT	0.90550	0.05802	0.22916	0.01106
STEADNCT	0.80486	0.08637	0.23863	0.04436

Factor Loadings for Various Sensory Tests and Tests of Motor Movement

Variable	Factor A VERGMOT	Factor B STMAZMOT	Factor C TAPMOT	Factor D PGTACTPT	Factor E LATDOMRM
LATDOMHR	0.01284	-0.03217	0.04723	0.00114	0.60890
LATDOMER	-0.05540	0.16675	0.02784	0.15194	0.53761
LATDOMFR	0.17404	-0.04712	0.00615	-0.01364	0.50226
LATDOMAR	0.05484	-0.00876	-0.13150	0.01629	0.46143
LATDOMNR	0.09037	-0.01816	-0.11355	-0.00599	-0.34263
TPTOTT	0.02695	0.06245	0.17885	0.42184	0.15871
TPTMEMT	-0.18891	0.30679	0.02990	0.40347	0.12974
TPTLOCT	-0.11204	0.26327	0.09646	0.49136	0.03386
FINTAPDT	0.02676	0.06153	0.69236	0.10901	0.07772
FINTAPNT	0.06356	0.09299	0.74242	0.15238	0.03175
FOOTAPDT	0.11667	0.17445	0.66254	0.16374	0.03249
FOOTAPNT	0.17652	0.22661	0.74927	0.21852	-0.11706
MAZEDTTT	0.21550	0.43083	0.14674	0.21507	0.07550
MAZENTTT	0.29961	0.53335	0.28719	0.33473	0.04038
VERGDTTT	0.82824	0.11122	0.15838	0.12697	0.07908
VERGNTTT	0.78813	0.09167	0.10523	0.19834	-0.01758
TACTFDT	0.18468	0.13316	0.16773	0.48628	0.08693
TACTFNT	0.26480	0.15286	0.11344	0.44982	0.12327
TACTFDET	0.04885	0.12959	-0.10038	0.35669	-0.14223
TACTFNET	0.07972	0.03163	0.00822	0.36334	0.03972
STEADDTT	0.03501	0.83987	0.12799	-0.00771	0.01718
STEADNTT	0.07107	0.80863	0.13376	0.11669	-0.01273
PEGDT	0.14382	0.25953	0.32219	0.50318	0.21509
PEGNT	0.06935	0.26969	0.27160	0.52067	0.18566
PEGDNT	-0.01195	0.04263	0.05892	0.10170	0.00885
PEGNNT	-0.01188	0.05936	0.03773	0.05772	-0.03083
FINGAGDT	0.09952	-0.07953	0.09683	0.45594	-0.09247
FINGAGNT	0.09424	-0.15341	0.08207	0.43003	-0.07950

APPENDIX 5

COMPARISON OF ALL SUBJECTS IN THE EIGHT GROUPS IN ONE-WAY ANOVAS
AND NEWMAN-KEULS MULTIPLE COMPARISONS

TEST	1[1]	2	3	4	5	6	7	8	F-ratio	df
PRFINTOT		[2]								
WISCPIQ	107.5	102.1+	102.3+	100.0+	109.2	103.7+	105.4	97.8+	3.019**	7,247
MATRST	54.8	49.2	51.9	50.6	54.6	49.7	54.1	50.3	1.708	7,214
DEVDRAWT	57.9	53.5+	52.2+	52.1+	55.4	53.0+	52.7+	51.6+	2.112*	7,247
CATOTT	54.3	51.8	51.6	51.8	54.4	48.7	51.3	49.7	1.434	7,215
ACADTOT										
WRARSS	94.3	87.4+	90.3+	78.1+	85.9+	93.1+	88.8+	92.9	6.437**	7,243
WRASSS	91.8	86.9+	89.2	79.0+	85.6+	87.9+	88.2+	87.7+	3.967**	7,241
WRAASS	97.6	90.8	92.2	92.9	91.9	92.6	92.2	89.1	1.989	7,246
VRBINTOT										
WISCVIQ	100.9	93.9+	90.0+	88.6+	100.1	98.8	97.3	96.8+	5.09**	7,245
PEABIQ	100.3	89.1+	80.1+	72.6+	102.6	97.9	97.9	91.8+	6.401**	7,219
PERCTOTA										
MCANSCAL	36.0	32.3+	32.3+	29.1+	37.5	36.3	33.2	33.8	3.628**	7,130
BOSTONT	53.0	46.6+	47.9	41.5+	54.3	53.2	49.4	52.2	4.266**	7,184
PGTACTPT										
TPTOTT	46.7	49.2	54.4+	52.9+	53.8+	52.0+	56.1+	47.2	3.249**	7,194
TPTMEMT	50.4	48.3	50.8	51.6	54.0	51.0	50.4	45.0	1.773	7,196
TPTLOCT	52.9	45.8	49.9	51.3	50.4	52.5	50.5	48.2	1.394	7,194

1. Numbers refer to comparison groups: 1 (French immersion); 2 (anglophones in francophone schools); 3 (ethnic groups in anglophone schools); 4 (francophones in francophone schools); 5 (reading disability); 6 (hyperactive); 7 (behaviour and personality problems); 8 (minimal brain dysfunction).
2. +refers to the significant difference by the Newman-Keul's test. All significant multiple comparisons noted refer to a comparison with the French immersion group.

*p<.05)for the overall F-ratio in the one-way ANOVAS.
**p<.01)

TEST	1	2	3	4	5	6	7	8	F-ratio	df
PEGDT	54.7	52.2	51.5	52.8	52.2	54.0	54.5	48.4+	3.432**	7,246
PEGNT	53.4	50.8	51.8	54.1	52.8	53.4	53.6	47.2+	3.273**	7,245
TACTFDT	50.6	49.5	50.1	52.5	53.6	52.5	53.8	48.4+	1.737	7,244
TACTFNT	52.5	49.5	50.4	53.5	54.4	51.3	52.9	48.3+	2.248*	7,244
TACTFDET	53.0	50.6	52.7	48.8	52.6	52.3	52.5	48.5+	1.957	7,244
TACTFNET	52.1	50.0	52.0	50.7	52.5	50.2	53.3+	46.8+	2.614*	7,244
FINGAGDT	51.1	50.3	49.8	51.7	49.3	49.6	55.2+	43.2+	3.878**	7,244
FINGAGNT	48.5	48.8	50.3	53.9	47.5	47.8	50.3	46.5	1.797	7,244
LATDOMRM										
LATDOMHR	5.2	5.4	6.7	6.5	5.3	6.0	5.6	5.0	2.184*	7,248
LATDOMER	1.0	1.2	1.3	1.3	1.2	1.1	1.1	0.8	1.196	7,242
LATDOMFR	1.6	1.8	1.9	1.9	1.6	1.6	1.8	1.5	1.061	7,248
LATDOMAR	6.6	6.2	6.2	5.9	5.1	6.7	5.8	3.1	2.275*	7,246
LATDOMNR	20.0	16.6	13.7	13.4	17.2	17.2	14.5	20.6	1.826	7,230
STEADCT										
STEADDCT	52.4	49.8	47.4+	46.1+	53.4	50.0	53.8	50.3	2.503*	7,236
STEADNCT	50.0	49.0	47.8	45.9	52.6	50.7	51.7	48.0	1.368	7,233
LATDOMLM										
LATDOMHL	1.8	1.5	0.3	0.5	1.7	1.0	1.4	1.9	2.098*	7,248
LATDOMEL	0.8	0.6	0.5	0.7	0.8	0.7	0.7	0.9	0.816	7,242
LATDOMFL	0.7	0.7	0.4	0.7	0.7	0.6	0.8	0.8	0.736	7,248
LATDOMAL	3.3	3.7	3.7	3.9	4.9	3.2	4.0	6.8	2.344*	7,246
LATDOMNL	24.6	26.7	28.1	29.8	22.2	23.5	22.6	27.8	1.196	7,229

APPENDIX 6

COMPARISON OF EIGHT RESTRICTED AGE AND FSIQ SUB-SAMPLES IN ONE-WAY ANOVAS
AND NEWMAN-KEULS MULTIPLE COMPARISONS

TEST	1[1].	2	3	4	5	6	7	8	F-ratio	df
PRFINTOT										
WISCPIQ	104.6	104.2	104.6	102.1	102.8	104.1	101.6	95.5	1.828	7,114
MATRST	54.3	48.6	55.8	50.6	50.6	48.9	50.3	46.9	1.601	7,104
DEVDRAWT	55.5	55.6	53.2	55.7	54.9	53.0	52.0	50.0	1.240	7,114
CATOTT	54.6	50.2	52.4	53.6	55.2	48.3	49.3	49.9	1.323	7,107
ACADTOT										
WRARSS	88.9	84.7+[2].	91.9	80.9+	86.0	91.6	87.0	88.9	2.095*	7,113
WRASSS	87.2	89.8	89.0	80.7	86.6	88.6	88.3	84.9	1.948	7,114
WRAASS	95.1	92.5	95.7	96.1	92.6	89.8	92.2	88.8	1.235	7,114
VRBINTOT										
WISCVIQ	96.1	92.5	93.6+	89.7+	97.7+	95.4	93.1	95.9	1.139	7,114
PEABIQ	99.7	85.1+	93.8+	73.2+	103.6+	93.9+	92.4+	90.7+	4.506**	7,106
PERCTOTA										
MCANSCAL	35.4	33.3+	35.0	29.1+	36.4	34.8	32.2	33.0	1.949	7,84
BOSTONT	53.6	47.6+	50.2	40.7+	51.7	52.5	47.3+	52.6	2.421*	7,97
PGTACTPT										
TPTTOT	44.9	46.1	53.2+	55.7+	53.1+	51.7+	55.8+	43.5	3.710**	7,95
TPTMEMT	49.9	47.8	47.2	53.5	52.6	53.0	48.6	45.2	1.305	7,96
TPTLOCT	51.3	46.2	48.5	53.2	50.2	53.0	46.5	46.2	1.081	7,96

[1]. Numbers refer to comparison grous: 1 (French immersion); 2 (anglophones in francophone schools); 3 (ethnic groups in anglophone schools); 4 (francophones in francophone schools); 5 (reading disability); 6 (hyperactive); 7 (behaviour and personality problems); 8 (minimal brain dysfunction).
[2]. +refers to the significant difference by the Newman-Keul's test. All significant multiple comparisons noted refer to a comparison with the French immersion group.
 *p<.05) for the overall F-ratio in the one-way ANOVAS.
**p<.01)

TEST	1[1]	2	3	4	5	6	7	8	F-ratio	df
PEGDT	53.5	53.2	53.6	52.7	50.5	53.6	54.3	46.1+	2.722*	7,113
PEGNT	53.7	51.2	49.7	53.4	52.3	52.6	53.2	44.3+	2.543*	7,113
TACTFDT	51.0	50.7	51.8	48.5	52.3	53.1	53.7	45.2	1.535	7,112
TACTFNT	54.0	49.5	52.4	49.9	52.3	51.4	52.3	45.8	1.655	7,112
TACTFDET	54.4	51.1	53.3	51.4	52.7	51.9	52.7	50.0	0.911	7,112
TACTFNET	50.9	47.0	53.6	51.8	52.4+	49.0	53.3	47.1	1.795	7,112
FINGAGDT	51.1	52.8	52.5	51.8	42.6+	49.3	54.8	39.0+	4.237**	7,114
FINGAGNT	47.6	49.6	53.2	54.5	44.0	47.3	51.5	44.5	1.967	7,114
LATDOMRM										
LATDOMHR	5.2	5.3	6.8	6.6	5.7	6.1	5.2	4.8	1.204	7,114
LATDOMER	0.9	1.0	1.1	1.1	1.1	1.3	0.9	0.5	1.553	7,109
LATDOMFR	1.6	1.7	2.1	1.6	1.9	1.7	1.7	1.4	0.725	7,114
LATDOMAR	7.4	6.5	6.5	4.2	5.2	7.0	5.7	3.3	1.516	7,112
LATDOMNR	18.4	19.8	12.8	12.1	17.0	16.1	12.4	20.3	1.284	7,109
STEADCT										
STEADDCT	52.8	48.8	50.2	48.5	56.1	51.5	52.6	49.8	1.158	7,109
STEADNCT	50.2	46.6	48.7	49.2	55.1	50.9	50.1	44.8	1.220	7,108
LATDOMLM										
LATDOMHL	1.8	1.6	0.2	0.4	1.3	0.8	1.8	2.1	1.149	7,114
LATDOMEL	0.9	0.8	0.8	0.9	0.8	0.7	0.8	1.3	0.764	7,109
LATDOMFL	0.6	0.8	0.2	0.6	0.7	0.5	0.9	0.6	0.560	7,114
LATDOMAL	2.5	3.4	3.5	5.5	4.8	2.7	4.1	6.7	1.630	7,112
LATDOMNL	23.9	30.7	30.1	27.8	19.1	25.1	18.4	25.1	1.263	7,109

APPENDIX 7

PEABODY PICTURE VOCABULARY TEST DATA

TABLE 1

Frequency and Percent of Various Chronological Age (CA) and Mental Age (MA) Relationships in the Four Comparison Groups

	French Immersion- French Immersion		French Immersion- English		English- English		French Immersion Success	
	Frequency	%	Frequency	%	Frequency	%	Frequency	%
First testing								
MA ≥ CA	7	70	3	50	6	100	5	71.4
MA < CA	3	30	3	50	0	0	2	28.6
Follow-up testing								
MA ≥ CA	8	80	5	71.4	6	100	3	42.9
MA < CA	2	20	2	28.6	0	0	4	57.1

TABLE 2

Mean MA Scores at First Testing and Follow-Up Testing and Differences Between These Means for the Four Comparison Groups

Testing	Peabody MA			
	French Immersion- French Immersion	French Immersion- English	English- English	French Immersion Success
First	8.583	6.986	8.333	7.5
Follow-up	9.567	8.774	10.083	8.154
Difference	.984	1.788	1.750	.654

TABLE 3

Means for Peabody B-A at First Testing and Follow-up Testing for the Four Comparison Groups

Testing	Peabody B-A			
	French Immersion- French Immersion	French Immersion- English	English- English	French Immersion Success
First	40.375	30.67	34.83	1.25
Follow-up	9.75	8.42	10.33	0

APPENDIX 8

DISCREPANCY SCORES BETWEEN ACHIEVEMENT TEST SCORES AND BOTH ACTUAL AND EXPECTED GRADE LEVELS AT FIRST TESTING AND AT RETESTING FOR INDIVIDUAL SUBJECTS IN THE THREE FRENCH IMMERSION DIFFICULTY GROUPS AND THE FRENCH IMMERSION SUCCESS GROUP

186

French immersion-French immersion difficulty group

	FIRST TESTING					FOLLOW-UP TESTING				
	Discrepancy Scores Actual Grade Level		Discrepancy Scores Expected Grade Level			Discrepancy Scores Actual Grade Level		Discrepancy Scores Expected Grade Level	
Subj.	Reading	Spell.	Arith.	Reading	Spell.	Arith.	Reading	Spell.	Arith.	Reading	Spell.	Arith.
1	-0.1	0	-0.4	-0.1	0	-0.4						
2	0	0.8	0.5	0	0.8	0.5	-0.1	0.6	1.1	-0.1	0.6	1.1
3	-0.2	-0.5	0	-0.2	-0.5	0						
4	0.6	0.8	-0.9	1.6	1.8	0.1	0.9	1.3	0	1.9	2.3	1.0
5	1.4	1.4	0.7	1.4	1.4	0.7	1.9	2.5	0.8	1.9	2.5	0.8
6	0.3	0.6	0.3	0.3	0.6	0.3	-1.1	0.7	1.1	-1.1	0.7	1.1
7	0.4	0.3	-0.3	1.4	1.3	0.7	1.3	0.9	0.7	2.3	1.9	1.7
8	0.4	1.0	-0.3	0.4	1.0	-0.3	0.3	1.6	0.4	0.3	1.6	0.4
9	0.1	0.2	-0.6	0.5	0.6	-0.2	-0.8	-0.1	-0.1	-0.4	0.3	0.3
10	-0.6	-0.2	0.2	-0.6	-0.2	0.2	-0.1	0.2	0	-0.1	0.2	0
11	0.8	0.4	0	0.8	0.4	0						
12	-0.7	0.2	0.5	-0.7	0.2	0.5	-0.2	0.9	-0.6	-0.1	1.0	-0.5
13	-0.9	-0.5	-1.1	-0.9	-0.5	-1.1						
14	0.7	0.5	-0.3	2.7	2.5	1.7						
15	-0.3	0.1	0	-0.3	0.1	0	0.2	0.1	0.1	0.2	0.1	0.1

| | FIRST TESTING ||||||| FOLLOW-UP TESTING |||||||
| | Discrepancy Scores Actual Grade Level ||| Discrepancy Scores Expected Grade Level ||| Discrepancy Scores Actual Grade Level ||| Discrepancy Scores Expected Grade Level |||
	Reading	Spell.	Arith.	Reading	Spell.	Arith.	Reading	Spell.	Arith.	Reading	Spell.	Arith.
Subj.	French immersion-English difficulty group											
1	0.7	-0.2	0.5	0.7	-0.2	0.5	0.8	1.7	0.1	0.8	1.7	0.1
2	0.5	0.6	0.5	1.5	1.6	1.5	1.8	2.1	1.5	2.8	3.1	2.5
3	0.1	0.5	-0.2	0.1	0.5	-0.2	0.1	-0.6	0.1	0.1	-0.6	0.1
4	0.7	0.3	-0.1	0.7	0.3	-0.1	-0.5	-0.4	-0.3	0.5	0.6	0.7
5	0.4	0.6	0.7	0.4	0.6	0.7	0.2	0.7	0	1.2	1.7	1.0
6	0.3	0.4	-0.4	0.3	0.4	-0.4	-1.4	-0.8	0.1	-1.4	-0.8	0.1
7	0.3	0.5	0.4	0.3	0.5	0.4	0.6	1.3	1.0	0.6	1.3	1.0
Subj.	English-English difficulty group											
1	0.6	1.3	0.7	0.6	1.3	0.7	-1.7	-0.1	-0.3	-0.7	0.9	0.7
2	0.2	1.3	0.1	0.2	1.3	0.1	-0.4	0.2	0.3	0.6	1.2	1.3
3	0.5	0.6	0	0.5	0.6	0	-0.4	0.2	0.3			
4	0.7	0.5	0.4	0.7	0.5	0.4	-1.1	-0.3	0.3	0.1	0.7	0.7
5	0.1	0.6	0.5	0.9	1.6	1.5						
6	1.4	1.4	0.3	2.4	2.4	1.3	1.1	1.6	0	2.1	2.6	1.9
7	0.9	0.8	-0.1	1.9	1.8	0.9	1.4	1.1	-0.1	3.4	3.1	1.9

	FIRST TESTING						FOLLOW-UP TESTING					
	Discrepancy Scores Actual Grade Level			Discrepancy Scores Expected Grade Level			Discrepancy Scores Actual Grade Level			Discrepancy Scores Expected Grade Level		
Subj.	Reading	Spell.	Arith.	Reading	Spell.	Arith.	Reading	Spell.	Arith.	Reading	Spell.	Arith.

English-English difficulty group (cont'd.)

Subj.	Reading	Spell.	Arith.	Reading	Spell.	Arith.	Reading	Spell.	Arith.	Reading	Spell.	Arith.
8	-0.1	0.3	-0.6	0.9	1.3	0.4	0.1	0.3	-0.6	1.1	1.3	0.4
9	-0.3	-0.8	-0.3	-0.3	-0.8	-0.3						
10	0.3	0.4	0.8	0.3	0.4	0.8						

French immersion success group

1	-1.0	-0.7	-1.2	-1.0	-0.7	-1.2	0.6	0.7	-0.4	0.6	0.7	-0.4
2	-1.0	-1.0	0.4	-1.0	-1.0	0.4	-2.1	-3.5	0.2	-2.1	-3.5	0.2
3	-4.1	0.4	0.1	-4.2	0.4	0.1						
4	-2.7	-0.7	0.4	-2.7	-0.7	0.4	-1.5	-0.5	1.4	-1.5	-0.5	1.4
5	-0.1	-0.1	-0.3	-0.1	-0.1	-0.3	0.6	0.2	0.1	0.6	0.2	0.1
6	-0.7	-0.1	-0.6	-0.7	-0.1	-0.6	-0.2	0.1	-0.3	-0.2	0.1	-0.3
7	-2.2	-1.9	-0.5	-3.2	-2.9	-1.5	-2.7	-2.5	0.6	-3.7	-3.5	-1.6
8	-1.1	-1.2	-0.8	-1.1	-1.2	-0.8	-0.3	0.3	-0.6	-0.3	0.3	-0.6

APPENDIX 9

FREQUENCY AND PERCENT OF SUBJECTS IN EACH OF THE FOUR COMPARISON GROUPS SCORING
BELOW AND AT OR ABOVE ACTUAL AND EXPECTED GRADE LEVELS ON THE WRAT

	French Immersion-French Immersion				French Immersion-English				English-English				French Immersion Success			
	Below		At/Above		Below		At/Above		Below		At/Above		Below		At/Above	
	Freq.	%	Freq.	%	Freq.	%	Freq.	%	Freq.	%	Freq.	%	Freq.	%	Freq.	%
Actual Grade Level: First Testing																
Reading	6	60	4	40	7	100	0	0	5	83.3	1	16.7	0	0	7	100
Spelling	9	90	1	10	6	85.7	1	14.3	6	100	0	0	0	0	7	100
Arithmetic	5	50	5	50	4	57.1	3	42.9	3	50	3	50	2	28.6	5	71.4
Actual Grade Level: Follow-up Testing																
Reading	5	50	5	50	5	71.4	2	28.6	3	50	3	50	2	28.6	5	71.4
Spelling	9	90	1	10	4	57.1	3	42.9	4	66.6	2	33.3	4	57.1	3	42.9
Arithmetic	6	60	4	40	5	71.4	2	28.6	2	33.3	4	66.6	3	42.9	4	57.1
Expected Grade Level: First Testing																
Reading	6	60	4	40	7	100	0	0	6	100	0	0	0	0	7	100
Spelling	9	90	1	10	6	85.7	1	14.3	6	100	0	0	0	0	7	100
Arithmetic	7	70	3	30	4	57.1	3	42.9	5	83.3	1	16.7	2	28.6	5	71.4
Expected Grade Level: Follow-up Testing																
Reading	5	50	5	50	6	85.7	1	14.3	5	83.3	1	16.7	2	28.6	5	71.4
Spelling	10	100	0	0	5	71.1	2	28.6	6	100	0	0	4	57.1	3	42.7
Arithmetic	8	80	2	20	7	100	0	0	6	100	0	0	3	42.7	4	57.1

APPENDIX 10

INDIVIDUAL DIFFERENCE SCORES BETWEEN WRAT DISCREPANCY SCORES AT FIRST TESTING AND FOLLOW-UP TESTING FOR (A) ACTUAL GRADE LEVEL AND (B) EXPECTED GRADE LEVEL

	Part A (actual)			Part B (expected)	
Reading	Spelling	Arithmetic	Reading	Spelling	Arithmetic

French immersion-French immersion

-.1[1]	.2	-.6	-.1	.2	-.6
-.3	-.5	-.9	-.3	-.5	-.1
-.5	-1.1	-.1	-.5	-1.1	-.1
1.4	-.1	-.8	.8	-.1	-.8
-.6	-.6	-1.0	-.9	-.6	-1.0
.1	-.6	-.7	.1	-.6	-.7
.9	.3	-.5	.8	.3	-.5
-.5	-.4	.2	-.5	-.4	.2
-.5	-.7	1.1	-.6	.1	1.0
-.5	0	-.1	-.5	0	-.1

French immersion-English

-.1	-1.9	.4	-.1	-1.0	.4
-1.3	-.5	-1.0	-1.3	-1.2	-1.0
0	1.1	-.3	0	1.1	-.3
1.2	.7	.2	.2	-.3	-.8
.2	-.1	.7	-.8	-1.0	.3
1.7	1.2	-.5	1.1	1.4	-.5
-.3	-.8	-.6	-.3	-.8	.6

[1] A negative difference score indicates better performance at first testing. A positive difference score indicates better performance at follow-up testing.

	Part A (actual)			Part B (expected)	
Reading	Spelling	Arithmetic	Reading	Spelling	Arithmetic

English-English

Reading	Spelling	Arithmetic	Reading	Spelling	Arithmetic
1.9	1.4	.4	.9	.4	- .6
.9	.4	- .3	.1	- .6	-1.3
1.8	.8	.1	- .6	- .2	- .3
.3	- .2	.3	.3	- .2	- .6
- .5	- .3	0	-1.5	-1.4	-1.0
- .2	0	0	- .2	0	0

French immersion success

Reading	Spelling	Arithmetic	Reading	Spelling	Arithmetic
-1.6	-1.4	- .8	-1.6	-1.4	- .8
1.1	2.5	.2	1.1	2.5	.2
-1.2	- .2	-1.0	-1.2	- .2	-1.0
- .7	- .3	- .4	- .7	- .3	- .4
- .5	- .2	- .3	- .5	- .2	- .3
.5	.6	-1.1	.5	.6	.1
- .8	-1.5	- .2	- .8	-1.5	- .2